HEGEL

About the Author

Dr. Franz Wiedmann, like Hegel, was born in Stuttgart. He studied philosophy, theology, and education at the universities of Tübingen and Munich. After teaching at the University of Munich, he became Professor of the History of Philosophy at the Philosophical-Theological Institute at Dillingen and has been head of its philosophy department since 1966. He is the author of numerous articles and books on philosophical themes.

HEGEL

An Illustrated Biography

by Franz Wiedmann

Translated from the German by
Joachim Neugroschel

PEGASUS NEW YORK

Library of Congress Catalogue Card Number 68-21037

Contents

1 **HEGEL'S YOUTH IN STUTTGART—9**
Family and home—Schooling—Swabian mentality

2 **THE SEMINARY OF TÜBINGEN—16**
Study of philosophy and theology—Hegel, Hölderlin, and Schelling—
Enthusiasm for Rousseau—Master's Degree in philosophy and theological examination

3 **A PRIVATE TUTOR IN BERNE AND FRANKFURT—24**
Theological and political studies—The death of Hegel's father

4 **THE YEARS IN JENA—31**
Privatdozent and Professor of Philosophy—*The Phenomenology of Mind*—
The Battle of Jena—Editing the *Bamberger Zeitung*

5 **THE HEADMASTER IN NUREMBERG—41**
Hegel as a teacher—Marriage to Marie von Tucher—Hegel's sons—
The Science of Logic—Three offers of professorships

6 **HEIDELBERG—55**
The Encyclopedia of the Philosophical Sciences—First disciples

7 **BERLIN: THE CULMINATION—62**
Minister zum Altenstein offers Hegel a professorship—Inaugural lecture—Polemics against Schleiermacher—Hegel as Prussian philosopher
laureate: *Outline of the Philosophy of Law*—Lectures on the Philosophy of
History—Aesthetics and philosophy of religion—Hegel and Goethe—
Hegel's travels in letters to his wife—The household in Berlin—Hotho
on Hegel—Estrangement from Schelling—Birthday celebration, 1826—
Hegel's speeches as President of the University—Last political work—
Illness, death, funeral

8   THE HEGELIAN SCHOOLS—*112*
   Opponents and followers—The "right wing" and the "left wing"—
   David Friedrich Strauss—The *Halle Yearbooks* and Ludwig Feuerbach

9   HEGEL AND MARXISM—*122*
   Marx and Engels—The reversal of Hegel

CHRONOLOGY—*131*

NOTES—*133*

BIBLIOGRAPHY—*135*

INDEX—*137*

SOURCES OF ILLUSTRATIONS—*143*

HEGEL

1

Hegel's Youth in Stuttgart

Family and Home

In the sixteenth century, Protestants from Styria and Carinthia, the Austrian territory of Ferdinand II, fled to Württemberg, a Lutheran Duchy in southern Germany. One of these refugees, a pewterer named Johannes Hegel, settled in Grossbottwar, a town in the Swabian wine-growing district. He soon felt at home there and later was even elected mayor. Some of his descendants were vicars and deacons in Sindelfingen, Reutlingen, and Winnenden (Friedrich Schiller was baptized by a Pastor Hegel in Marbach, on November 11, 1759). Others became lawyers and town clerks. The grandfather of the philosopher Hegel was the high bailiff of Altenstein in the Black Forest. His son, Georg Ludwig, was a secretary in the revenue office and then an expeditionary councilor. On September 29, 1769, he married Maria Magdalena Fromm in Stuttgart. On August 27, 1770, they had a son, whom they christened Georg Wilhelm Friedrich.

At the time, the parents resided at 53 *Eberhardstrasse*, near relatives named Hauff;* a few doors down, Friedrich Schiller, then still a regimental doctor, lived in the house of Mrs. Vischer, a captain's widow. The house in which Hegel was born bears a bronze plaque by K. Donhoff; having withstood the devastation of World War II, the building still stands in the center of town. In 1776, the Hegel family moved to the so-called "wealthy suburb" near the "Sporting

---

*One of the Hauffs was Wilhelm, a well-known Swabian writer of short stories and novels. [Tr.]

The house in which Hegel was born: 53 Eberhard-strasse, Stuttgart.

Ground," west of *Königsstrasse;* this suburb has since become a non-residential downtown area full of banks and department stores.

Rödersche Gasse (now *Lange Strasse*) was right near the Latin School, the so-called Professorial House, and the *Gymnasium Illustre,* predecessor of the *Eberhard Ludwig Gymnasium.* Anything surviving the pickaxes of city planners was destroyed by air raids in 1943 and 1944. The house on *Lange Strasse,* with a commemorative tablet by Wilhelm Pelargus, no longer exists.[1]

Expeditionary Councilor Hegel had three children, of whom the eldest was greatly spoiled "because he was such a good pupil." The younger son, Georg Ludwig, became an officer, took part in the Russian Campaign, and died young; Christiane, the daughter, outlived her famous brother. During her service as governess in the employ of Count von Berlichingen, she contracted a nervous disorder; after a few years of tutoring French and needlework in Aalen, she finally had to enter Zwiefalten sanatorium. Her brother later sent her money from Berlin. Dr. Karl Eberhard Schelling (a brother of the philosopher Schelling) treated her medically, but she showed no improvement. In 1832, while visiting Bad Teinach, she committed suicide. A posthumously discovered letter of hers, addressed to Hegel's widow and dated January 7, 1832, contains the following recollections:

Schiller as military surgeon (painting by P. F. Hetch, 1782).

"Let me tell you whatever my poor physical and mental state allows me to gather together about my brother's childhood: At three, he was sent to German School and at five to Latin School, by which age he already knew the first declension and the Latin words belonging to it. He had been taught by our late mother, who was quite learned for a woman of her time and therefore exerted a great influence on his initial studies. In every class he was awarded a prize each year, since he was always one of the five best pupils; and from the age of ten to eighteen, he was always first in his section of the *Gymnasium*. When he was eight years old, his teacher Löffler, who was very fond of him and contributed a good deal to his subsequent education, gave him a copy of Shakespeare's dramatic works translated by Eschenburg, with the remark: "You won't understand them now, but you'll soon learn to understand them." This teacher had thus already seen the profundity in the boy, and I still recall that *The Merry Wives of Windsor* was the first play to appeal to my brother. Our father had gotten him private tutors quite early, which is mentioned in the encyclopedia and also holds true for his studies in Tübingen. When my brother was ten, father sent him to study geometry with Christian Duttenhofer, who was still alive at the time. Duttenhofer took the boy and several other youngsters surveying and taught them a little astronomy as well.

In confirmation class, the father confessor (later Prelate Grie-singer) was extremely satisfied with the boy's knowledge of religion. In 1783, bilious dysentery and bilious fever were raging in Stutt-gart, and the latter disease attacked our father, our mother, Hegel, and myself. No one could tell who of the first three would be the first to die; our dear mother succumbed. Hegel grew so ill that he developed angina, and we all despaired of his life; he recovered, but afterwards a large malignant ulcer formed behind his ear and he had to undergo a painful operation. I forgot to mention that at the age of six he had such a terrible case of the pox that even the doctor gave him up for lost, and Hegel was blind for several days. During his university period, he suffered from tertian ague for a long time, and therefore spent several months in our father's home, where on better days he perused the Greek Tragedies—his favorite reading matter—and studied botany. . . ."[2]

Schooling

A true model pupil, Hegel should have been sent to one of the *Little Seminaries,* which prepared students for the university, and for which Duke Christoph of Württemberg had converted a number of monasteries "for the aims and needs of young Protestants." But the plan did not work out, and so Hegel remained at the Stuttgart *Gymnasium.* Its curriculum gave top priority to the study of Greek and Roman classics. The students' "chief nourishment was the mar-row of Antiquity." Yet the school does not seem to have been so excellent as the Hegel biographies claim. There are dissenting opinions on the organization and the syllabus at the time Hegel was there:

"The lower *Gymnasium* . . . was corrupted by unbelievable abuses. The teachers—seven in all, and none of them specialists—received no salary and were therefore dependent on the tuition fees; thus they understandably desired to have as many pupils as possible (even sixty or more) and to hold on to them in some way or other for a year beyond the normal year. . . . As a result, the individual classes contained an uneven variety of pupils whose ages and knowl-edge were more disparate than anyone might dream. Their ages ran from four to nine and ten, whereas in the Upper *Gymnasium* eleven-year-olds studied next to twenty-year-olds. In addition there was no unified curriculum planning whatever for the individual subjects . . . every instructor taught according to his own will and on his own responsibility."[3]

At fifteen, Hegel began to keep a journal, partly in German and partly in Latin, "in an orderly quarto notebook of draft paper." The entries are unsystematic and usually concern incidents at school, his progress there, and his readings. Like the German novelist, Jean

Paul, he employed the "method of excerpting and abstracting." Thus, next to a section entitled *On Excerpting,* we find long passages from Sulzer's *A Brief Idea of Scholarship,* J. M. Schröckh's *Primer of Universal History,* Feder's *New Emil,* Kästner, Nicolai, and, last but not least, from the writings of Christian Garve, the sensitive German translator of Ferguson, Burke, and Adam Smith. Hegel's diary thus indicates that in his youth he became thoroughly familiar with eighteenth-century literature; this was probably why his own works reflected this tradition, utilizing its wealth of psychological and aesthetic insights.

In an entry dated Monday, January 1, 1787, he wrote: "This afternoon, I wanted to read just a little of *Sophie's Journey;* but then I couldn't put the book down."[4]

The book he meant was a novel, *Sophie's Journey from Memel to Saxony,* by Johann Thimotheus Hermes, Professor of Theology at Breslau. Schopenhauer, upon learning this in Karl Rosenkranz's biography of Hegel, triumphantly wrote to his pupil, K. Bähr: "My favorite book is Homer; Hegel's favorite is Sophie's Journey. . . ." Kuno Fischer, too, seems to hold Hegel's lapse of taste against him; he calls the novel "one of the worst and most tedious products of our literature." These "unassuming portrayals of the panorama of everyday life with its commonplace people, insipid prattle, and dull conviviality" impressed the young man, according to Fischer, simply because "there was something commonplace, oldish, philistine" about him "which was intellectually brought under control only with the gradual advance of his world of ideas. At the time no one would have guessed that in this unassuming adolescent . . . a profound thinker was hidden, who would one day struggle to the surface and emerge as the foremost philosopher of an epoch."[5]

Hegel certainly sounds a bit like an old fogy in his entry of Monday, June 27, 1785. The heads of the different classes were to appear as the *capita repraesentativa* before an assembly of the *Gymnasium* professors. "All they did was to urge us gravely to warn our comrades not to take part in wretched, dissolute card parties and the like. It seems that a group of young people, the males sixteen or seventeen years of age and the females eleven, twelve, etc., has made itself conspicuous; they go by the name of Bulldog Society, Laplanders, etc. The young sparks take the young ladies walking and fritter away their time in an abandoned fashion."[6]

After the death of his revered teacher, *Praeceptor* Löffler, Hegel wrote about their close relationship:

He was [the] most upright and equitable of men. His main concern was to be of help to his pupils, himself, and the world. He was not low-minded like those who felt that since they were now earning their living they could stop studying as long as they managed to keep up with their humdrum classroom routine year after year. No! This was not the deceased's way of thinking. He knew the value of scholarship and the solace it brings in various states of fortune. How often and how content and cheerful did he sit with me in my beloved room or I in his. Few people were aware of his merits; it was a great misfortune· for this man that he had to work completely within his own sphere. And now he, too, has passed away. But the memory of him will be fixed in my heart eternally![7]

Swabian Mentality

Hegel's home, like that of every old, established family in Stuttgart up to the beginning of our century, was marked by Protestant Pietism. And thus Hegel was steeped in its theosophy and mysticism from childhood. His Swabian disposition was never rarefied—not even "in the element of the universal, the ether of thought and philosophy." Not only does the wine made on the banks of the Neckar have a different taste and mischievousness from that of the Rhineland, but the people too have their own distinct mentality. Reserved and uncommunicative, they conceal deep within themselves a quiet faculty for brooding and meditating. This is the source not only of their peculiar wit, their amiable sense of humor (not touched with irony or sarcasm), their heavy tongue, pensive speech and laborious articulation, but also of their gift for the apt image and vivid description so characteristic of Hegel's own style.[8] He kept the broad sing-song Swabian inflection even when teaching at the University of Berlin—like Schelling, who delighted his students every time he used the Swabian form *"äbbes"* for the High German *"etwas."* Hegel quite seriously believed that the Swabian dialect, with its inexhaustible modulatory possibilities, was most suited to philosophy.

In point of fact, the Swabian lowland had produced over the years an array of outstanding writers, philosophers, and theologians. A touchingly complacent song goes:

> *Der Schelling und der Hegel,*
> *Der Schiller und der Hauff,*
> *Das ist bei uns die Regel*
> *Und fällt uns gar nicht auf.*

This might be translated as:

> *Schelling and Hegel,*
> *Schiller and Hauff,*
> *It's all so normal for us*
> *That we don't even notice it.*

Most of these men started out in the Seminary of Tübingen *(Tübinger Stift)*, which Hegel entered in October 1788.

On graduating from the *Gymnasium*, Hegel delivered the valedictorian address on the rather out-of-the-way theme: "The Abortive State of Art and Scholarship in Turkey." The underlying intention of this fustian exercise was to demonstrate how much better it was to be educated at the Stuttgart *Gymnasium:* establishments of learning are neglected in Turkey, but here they flourish, "which we owe not only to Karl [the Duke] but pre-eminently to you, most honored gentlemen [the teachers]."[9]

As far as we know, Hegel never considered studying anything but theology. In a self-effacing application co-signed by his father, he asks for "most gracious" admission to "Your Highness's Theological Foundation in Tübingen." He promises to "study with all seriousness and zeal, but particularly to enter no profession other than *theologiam,* and constantly to work for and toward it with GOD'S grace, so that I may be of service in churches or schools to Your Highness, your Highness's Realm, as well as foreign governments and wherever your Highness may lend me or order me to be sent." The father promised to mortgage his property and conscientiously to urge and encourage his son to work diligently toward the goal of becoming a clergyman.[10]

2

The Seminary of Tübingen

Study of Philosophy and Religion

The University of Tübingen was small and insignificant when Hegel registered for the winter semester of 1788. The student body numbered some two or three hundred, most of them studying theology or planning to become *Gymnasium* teachers; those interested in medicine or law studied at the *Karlsschule* in Stuttgart. Tübingen was one of the numerous state universities whose primary aim was to prepare young men for service in the government, the church, or education. The philosophical faculty boasted of such professors as August F. Bök and Jakob Friedrich Abel (who had taught Schiller at the *Karlsschule*), and most important of all, the Orientalist C. F. Schnurrer, a scholar of European renown, who had met Rousseau in France. An alumnus and a theologian, he was director of the Seminary; he was somewhat stern, but his sincerity made him the most popular teacher there. The most prominent members of the theological faculty were Johann Friedrich Flatt, who lectured on ethics and the New Testament, and Gottlob Storr. Storr, an advocate of systematic theology, was undoubtedly the most renowned teacher on the staff.[11]

Hegel, as recipient of a ducal scholarship, lived in the Theological Seminary, which had been founded by Duke Ulrich in 1536 and had moved into the former Augustinian monastery in 1547. Julius Klaiber describes the site as follows:

"At the foot of the vine-covered rise on which the old fortress of Hohentübingen stands, right on the slopes of the Neckar, in the space between the hill and the river, Austin friars had built their monastery in a truly beautiful place: down below, at the wall of the monastery garden, the swift flowing river with willows on both shores; upstream, the verdant meadows, closed off by the lovely protrusion of the mountain; downstream, the brightly gleaming road with the city wall in front of it, leading to the stone bridge spanning the Neckar and to the Oesterberg crowning it; yet the Steinlach valley is lovely enough, opening as it does into a wide plain, and beyond it, above the bosky summits of the closer hills, the misty chain of the Alps and, in bold relief, the friendly silhouette of the mountain graced by the Salmendig chapel.

The old monastery had two parallel wings connected by a cloister; the back wing, resting against the mountain but separated by a deep moat from the higher street, contained the church with its choir facing east; the other wing, with the refectory and the cells above, stretched along the Neckar. This was how the building looked when the Seminary moved in." [12]

The Seminary scholars had a special uniform consisting of a lightweight black coat with white cuffs and collar, a costume that Hölderlin wore with a certain elegance, whereas Hegel's looked downright slovenly. The hours for study, recreation, and going out were strictly regulated and, like attendance at the lectures, were checked by assistants. A breach of discipline was punished by a so-called *carition*: the lunchtime wine-ration was withheld or—since few of the students ever drank the low-quality wine—a corresponding sum of money was docked. More serious infringements were punished by *incarceration*.

Unfortunately, transgressions against the rules seemed to constitute the only basis for evaluating the students, and great stress was laid on this method, even against the better judgment of the headmasters. For lack of anything else to go by, the total number of *caritions* and their quarterly entry in the so-called *Carentengatter* (from *quattuor*) determined the reports on the students—as if following rules could vouch for character. No wonder the superior students protested by frequent breaches of discipline. At first, Hegel's punishments (for cutting lectures, getting up late, or not attending prayers) stayed within reason. But on Saint Sebastian's Day (January 20) 1790, eighteen *caritions* were listed for him, and on February 12 he received a serious warning. A year later, the very same ill-omened Saint Sebastian's Day brought him two hours of detention. He returned to school an hour late, claiming "his pony had been injured"; actually, however, as the director preferred to assume, his two friends, Finck and Fallot, had ridden out to meet him without permission.

The semester reports by the tutors state that Hegel's aptitude and application are usually *ingenium bonum, diligens.* His *mores* are initially *boni,* but later merely *probi* or *recti,* and at one point even *languidi.*[13]

Hegel, Hölderlin, and Schelling

During the winter term of 1790–1791, Hölderlin wrote to his sister that Hegel and Märklin, who roomed with him, were in his class, "and the few others are a decent sort, including Breyer and Schelling." Hegel and Hölderlin were Schelling's seniors by five years. Of the three friends, who were to go their separate ways afterwards, Hegel was the prudent, older doctoral candidate, with no apparent trace of genius. "We would never have thought it of Hegel," said other schoolday friends upon hearing of his fame in Berlin. Being on the stout side, he didn't care much for fencing or horseback riding. The young ladies sneered at his slovenly attire, but they liked him for his bonhomie and his mental alertness. Whenever possible, Hegel would arrange a game of forfeits, and "a kiss would finally have to be granted him by graceful lips."[14] His ponderous ways made him seem older than he really was; in his dormitory, they nicknamed him "der Alte" (the old man). His friend Fallot drew a caricature of the nineteen-year-old in Hegel's

Tübinger Stift: *Seminary at Tübingen.*

Friedrich Hölderlin (pastel drawing by Hiemer).

album. It showed the adolescent skulking along on crutches, and the caption read: "God help the old man!"

On the other hand, Hegel was a well-liked participant at the frequent drinking bouts in Tübingen's cafés. Instead of preparing his theological coursework, he liked nothing better than to join the group of philosophizing wine sippers, take hearty doses of snuff, play Tarok, and make his audience laugh with his earthy, double-entendre jokes. Often, he would return to the Seminary quite late, and once the distraught dormitory senior supposedly called out to him: "Oh Hegel, you'll drink away what little intelligence you have!" J. H. Faber, who became minister of Oberstenfeld, recalls the evening that Hegel came home in a far from edifying condition and had to be hidden by him from the Seminary police.[15]

Enthusiasm for Rousseau

During his first few years at Tübingen, Hegel's expeditions into the realm of knowledge were at best random raids. He did read Plato, Kant, Schiller, Jacobi, Hemsterhuis, Montesquieu, and Herder, but when the Kantians at the Seminary formed a club, Hegel preferred not to join, claiming that he was totally involved in studying Rousseau. Significantly, he was more interested in practical matters at the time than in theories or metaphysics. In contrast to Hölderlin and Schelling, he was absorbed by political problems pertaining to an improvement of the status quo. Thus, Hölderlin wrote to Neuffer: "From the great Jean-Jacques I learned a bit about the rights of man, and on clear nights I devoted myself to Orion or Sirius and the divine twins Castor and Pollux." Hegel, on the other hand, who many years later is said to have shrugged off the starry night as an "ugly eczema," sat poring over Rousseau's writings. For him, the Frenchman was the great cultural politician; his concept of "volonté générale," that is, the supra-individual and collective will, as opposed to the "volonté de tous," the will of all, presaged the Hegelian and Romantic idea of the *Volksgeist,* the collective spirit of a people. If we can believe the account that Magister Leutwein (whom Rosenkranz referred to as a "run-down genius") gave Schwegler, Hegel did not appreciate metaphysics or Kant while he was at Tübingen:

"I don't really know whether, or to what extent, Hegel was changed by his last year here, during which he was not with me. But I have my doubts. At any rate, during the four years of our close association, metaphysics was not his cup of tea. His hero was Rousseau, whose *Émile, Contrat Social,* and *Confessions* he was constantly reading. Hegel thought he might thereby rid of himself of certain generally accepted prejudices and preconceived ideas, or 'shackles,' as he himself put it. The *Book of Job* gave him special pleasure because of its irregular, chaotic language of nature. On the whole, I thought him somewhat eccentric at times. His subsequent opinions only came to him abroad, for in Tübingen he wasn't even really familiar with Father Kant. And I, who at the time was engrossed in Kant's work and frequently talked about it with Schelling, Breyer, Flatt, Märklin, Duttenhoffer, Diez (a tutor and fierce Kantian), Hauber, *et al,* could get little response from Hegel to my conversations about Kant, Reinhold, or Fichte."[16]

A "Political Club" had been formed at Tübingen, and the most active members came from Montbeliard (Mömpelgard), a county across the Rhine, then still belonging to Württemberg. The students from Montbeliard, who were granted free board at the Seminary, represented the French element, and Hegel was friendly with most of them, especially Fallot and Billing from Colmar. Naturally, the main subject of their debates was the French Revolution. With youthful enthusiasm they hoped for an ethical rebirth of Europe after the Declaration of Human Rights. They read French newspapers, devoured the news, discussed events, and their fervor was so strong that one fine Sunday morning in the spring of 1791, the young enthusiasts of freedom went to a meadow just outside of Tübingen and, emulating the French, put up a liberty

Jean-Jacques Rousseau (painting by Allan Ramsay; Museum of Edinburgh).

tree. Afterwards they wrote *"Vive la liberté"* and *"Vive Jean-Jacques"* in one another's albums. News of the incident spread, and Duke Karl Eugen appeared in person; however, he very sensibly limited himself to a general censure of the spirit of opposition and disobedience. The chief ringleader, Wetzel, managed to escape to Strassburg in the nick of time.[17]

In the "outside world," revolutionary ideas had been circulating for a long while, the call for freedom was sounding, and Church and State were looked upon as "reservoirs of despotism." Rousseau's "gospel" had begun to exert its influence, traditional theology (especially the concept of divine inspiration for the Bible) was eliciting skepticism, and Kant's Critiques seemed to have demolished the old system of metaphysics. Criticism and opposition were now astir among the students of Tübingen, who realized that their university shut out all that was new while striving to preserve the "good old spirit" against the age of enlightenment.

However, we must not overlook one fact: neither Hegel nor Schelling ultimately became "revolutionaries" in the usual sense. In later years, they witnessed the true blossoming of the revolutionary spirit (through the German *Burschenschaften,* that is, fraternities) but never responded to these ideas. Instead, they became guardians of the status quo and, in the conservative spirit, they advocated

the value of historical traditions. Hegel became the Prussian political philosopher, whereas Schelling tried to preserve the "Christian
element" and bring about its renascence. Hegel's Tübingen period
may thus seem somewhat out of character, but it would be wrong
to view it as a minor episode in his life. In point of fact, those
years brought decisions of far-reaching consequence.[18]

We do not know why Hegel changed his mind about becoming
a minister. He may have been motivated less by an aversion toward
theology or the customs of the Seminary (the compulsory attendance
at prayers and church services, the ignoble forms of punishment in
a time of great changes and liberal ideas) and more by ill feelings
about what he considered unfair treatment at the hands of his
mentors. Unfortunately, our only source is once again the aforementioned Magister Leutwein:

"Hegel was one of the five *Gymnasium* graduates sent to Tübingen
to study under Renz, the first in his class according to the Stuttgart *Gymnasium*'s grading. The second-ranking student was also
from Stuttgart: Märklin, who afterwards became the superintendent-
general of Heilbronn and with whom I was on close terms. But
soon Hegel was ranked below Märklin; this was due either to the
tutors, or—more likely—to the inspectors, who may, among other
things, have been showing deference to Märklin's uncle (subsequently deputy-superintendent in Denkendorf). But Hegel's bohemian
ways had at least supplied them with a pretext, and his academic
diligence as well as his attendance at lectures did not exactly recommend him. There was something desultory about him, and I occasionally told him as much straight to his face. Furthermore, he
had not scorned to attend convivial gatherings, at which sacrifices
were offered to Bacchus. In short, Märklin, the more orderly of
the two, was ranked third in his doctoral class and Hegel fourth.

This demeaning inferior ranking left a permanent scar in Hegel's
heart, and no one knows this better than I, although Hegel did his
best to hide it from the world; this was in all certainty the secret
spring precipitating the alteration in him after all those years of
study. For previously, his father's opposition had stood in his way.
An independent need of a new philosophy was surely not yet the
cause. Had he remained third in his class, Berlin would certainly
never have seen him, nor would he have provided the German
Fatherland with so much material for discussion."[19]

Master's Degree in Philosophy and Theological Examinations

A two-year study of philosophy at Tübingen led to the *pro
magistro* disputation (the master's degree being equivalent to the
Doctor of Philosophy of other universities). This was followed by

a three-year course in theology, terminating with the *Dissertation pro candidatura examinis consitorialis*. In 1790, offering two original *specimina* (small scholarly essays), Hegel presented himself for the Master's Examination, which was given annually in September. Under the supervision of professors of the Faculty of Philosophy and in the presence of opposing tutors, a dissertation written by one of the professors was to be defended. Hegel, together with his fellow candidates Finck, Autenrieth, and Hölderlin, sustained the thesis of a paper on ethics by Professor Bök, *De limite officiorum* (On the Limits of Duty), and officially received his Master's Degree on September 27, 1790, in the great hall of the Aula Nova (today's Alte Aula near the Seminary church). The theological examination began in June 1793. Hegel and eight other candidates defended Chancellor Lebret's dissertation on a theme taken from the ecclesiastical history of Württemberg. The consistorial examination took place after the summer holidays on September 20, 1793.

The final certificate given to Hegel reads: *"Studia theologia non neglexit, orationem sacram non sine studio elaboravit, in recitando non magnus orator visus. Philologiae non ignarus, philosophiae multam operam impendit."* * E. Zeller, in his essay of 1845,[20] deliberately changed "multam" ("much") to "nullam" ("no"), which R. Hayn accepted without question for his biography of 1857: "His teachers gave him a certificate . . . which described him as a man with fine aptitudes, but of mediocre effort and knowledge, a poor speaker and an idiot in philosophy."[21]

After passing his examination, Hegel returned to Stuttgart in fall of 1793 to convalesce from a fever. He took frequent walks to Cannstatt and discussed his future with the poet and litterateur, Gotthold Friedrich Stäudlin, the then thirty-five-year-old friend of Hölderlin.

---

*"He did not neglect theological studies and worked zealously at sacred oratory [but] in his delivery he was seen to be no great orator. Not ignorant of philology, he devoted much labor to philosophy."

3

A Private Tutor in Bern and Frankfurt

A Private Tutor in Berne and Frankfurt

In the summer of 1793, Carl Friedrich Steiger von Tschugg, a Berne patrician, was looking for a private tutor. A certain Herr von Rütte had suggested Hegel for this position. The directors of the Tübingen Seminary were apparently not to be consulted, for on November 10, 1793, Professor Schnurrer wrote to a Herr Scholl in Holland:

"Herr M. Hegel is to take his final examinations this fall and will thus be free to accept an out-of-town position. A bit of circumspection would do no harm. I rather doubt whether he has in the meantime learned to submit patiently to the sacrifices normally required of a private tutor, at least initially. Allegedly convalescing, he has spent most of this summer away from the Seminary, and his protracted sojourn at home, where he is probably treated better than his father, is very unlikely to prepare him for the life of a private tutor, which is not precisely what one may call free."[22]

In any event, a correspondence ensued with Herr Von Rütte during August and September, and Hegel apparently began his new work in early October 1793. It was quite customary for young scholars without money or patronage to become private tutors before planning their *habilitation* (a post-doctoral degree). Kant, Fichte, Herbart, and Hölderlin had similar positions for a number of years. The main advantages, apart from free board and lodging as well as a small stipend, were a certain amount of leisure for independent study and the chance of being introduced into society, where further contacts could be made.

We know surprisingly little about Hegel's position in Berne. His first extant letter (to Schelling), dated Christmas Eve 1794, marks the end of more than a year of silence: "I am by no means totally idle, but my overly heterogeneous and frequently interrupted occupation allows me no time for proper work."[23] A brief report to his absent patron concerning events in the house and on the estate implies that Hegel's duties were not limited to educating the children. He obviously had to tutor the seven-year-old son, Friedrich, two daughters, and a boy from Neufchatel; but the details are obscure.

Theological and Political Studies

Captain Steiger's father had been a highly cultivated man with a background in politics. Failing to be elected to the Town Council of Bern, he turned his back on politics and retired sullenly to his estate at Tschugg, where he devoted himself entirely to his studies. He had a marvelous library of philosophical, historical, and political works, which Hegel was allowed to use freely.[24] We know that the young tutor read Grotius, Hobbes, Hume, Leibniz, Locke, Machiavelli, Montesquieu, Shaftesbury, Spinoza, and Voltaire. As for his own work, he continued the investigations begun in Tübingen on *Popular Religion and Christianity* but was much more critical now. Hegel returned to Kant's works, studying and excerpting them (*Religion within the Limits of Reason Alone* had appeared in 1793); he bought the writings of Fichte and collected material for a *Philosophy of the Subjective Spirit.* For the period from late July to early August 1796, we have an extremely sober, pedantic, and matter-of-fact journal of a trip that he took through the Bernese Upper Alps with three Saxon tutors.

In his letters, he paid tribute to Schelling's publications but said nothing about his own systematic studies. Perhaps he didn't consider them worth mentioning in the same breath with the work of his younger friend, who was rapidly gaining renown. Hegel was following his own ideal very gradually, as was his nature: "Don't expect any comments from me on your work. I'm only an apprentice. I'm trying to study Fichte's *Grundlage* [*The Science of Knowledge,* 1794]. . . . My own work isn't worth talking about." (Letter of August 30, 1795). At the age of seventeen, Schelling had already put out an essay (in *Memorabilien*) on *Myths, Historical Fables, and Philosophemae of Ancient Times.* By 1796, he had independently worked out the *Standpoint of the Theory of Knowledge* and then *The Standpoint*

Johann Gottlieb Fichte (lithograph by Friedrich Burg).

of Natural Philosophy, and at the age of twenty-six he was to bring out his *System of Transcendental Idealism.*

The warm, friendly letters to Schelling and Hölderlin contain primarily reminiscences of old times together in Tübingen; Hegel, feeling totally cut off, asks Schelling for the latest news:

"How are thing otherwise in Tübingen? Nothing solid will ever come out of there until they get someone of Reinhold's or Fichte's sort. No other university perpetuates the old system so faithfully."[25]

A month later, his tone was even sharper:

"The things you say about the theological . . . Kantian *(si diis placet)* state of philosophy at Tübingen come as no surprise. Orthodoxy cannot be shaken so long as the professing thereof is tied to worldly advantages and woven into the totality of a State. These concerns are too strong [for orthodoxy] to be given up easily, and they exert their influence without our fully realizing it. As long as this is so [orthodoxy] will get the support of the whole tribe of parrots and scribes who are devoid of ideas or higher interests, and they're the biggest tribe of all. Whenever they read anything contrary to their convictions (if we want to do their verbiage the honor of calling it this) and manage to sense some truth in it, they say: "Yes, that's probably so." Then they go to bed, and in the morning they drink their coffee and pour it for others, as if nothing had happened. Otherwise, they put up with anything that's offered them and that keeps them in their humdrum system. But I think it would be interesting to interfere as much as possible with the ant-like industriousness of the theologians who gather critical building material for the fortification of their Gothic temple, to make things difficult for them, to deprive them of every loophole until they're at a complete loss for another and are forced to expose their weaknesses in broad daylight. But among the material they drag away from the Kantian pyre in order to prevent the burning of dogmatism, they always take a few live coals along; thus they help the spread of philosophical ideas . . . Hölderlin sometimes writes to me from Jena. He's attending Fichte's lecture course and describes him enthusiastically as a titan fighting for humanity and whose influence will most certainly not remain within the walls of the lecture hall. . . . Let the Kingdom of God come, and may our hands not lie idle in our laps! . . . Let reason and freedom remain our watchwords, and the invisible church our rallying point."[26]

On Schiller's recommendation, Hölderlin had spent a year as tutor in the home of Charlotte von Kalb; early in 1796, he had accepted a similar position in the home of Gontard, a banker in Frankfurt am Main. Hölderlin's ecstatic love for Frau Gontard— she was the Diotima in his lyrical novel *Hyperion*—was full of a burning enthusiasm for all beauty and greatness but was to end in catastrophe for both the poet and his lady.

On October 24, 1796, Hölderlin wrote to Hegel:

"You will recall that at the beginning of the summer I wrote to you about an excellent position and that I wished with all my heart, for your sake and mine, that you would come to the good people I spoke of. . . . The day before yesterday Herr Gogel came by quite unexpectedly and told me that if you were still free and interested in the position, he would be very pleased."

Hölderlin describes the job in glowing colors: Hegel would have his own room, 400 florins for traveling expenses, rich presents, excellent wine with his meals, and the company of a reasonable, unassuming family. He adds:

"Someone who has remained faithful to you in heart, memory, and mind, despite rather considerable changes in his situation and character, and who will be a closer and warmer friend to you than ever before and willingly and sincerely share every part of life with you—this person would be living quite nearby if you came here. Really, my dear friend, I need you, and I believe that you will need me as well."[27]

Hegel, missing the close contact he had had with his Seminary friends, and feeling forlorn and secluded, agreed happily:

"I can't tell you what joy [the letter] brought me, and even more the hope of seeing and embracing you soon. . . . As sorry as I am not to be able to start out right away, I can't possibly leave the house I'm in before December or arrive in Frankfurt before mid-January."[28]

Hölderlin sensed that the position in Berne had deprived Hegel of his "well-known, ever-cheerful frame of mind" but assured his friend that only a few days together would rejuvenate both of them and once again made the new job sound tempting: "Elementary teaching may often oppress the mind, but you'll be happier instructing the boys than studying State and Church in their present condition."[29]

En route, Hegel spent a few days in Stuttgart with his parents; according to his sister, he seemed rather melancholy and lost in thought. In mid-January 1797 he became tutor in the Gogel household in Frankfurt. His fervent desires were now to be realized: "A rich literary library," greater leisure, and more contact with friends. And Hölderlin was equally thankful for the new opportunity of their being together. "Hegel's company," he wrote to Neuffer, "is very beneficial to me. I like calm intellectuals, because they help a person to get his bearings when he does not know where he stands with regard to himself and the world."

From the very first, Hegel felt better than ever before in his life. "Here in Frankfurt, I am once again becoming a part of the world," he told Nanette Endel, a childhood friend.[30] Above all, he managed to write lengthy papers and preliminary studies for his system. The fragments collected by Nohl under the title, *The Spirit of Christianity and Its Destiny,* dealt with a tragic idea of destiny and were profoundly influenced by Hölderlin's mental illness, which Hegel was obliged to witness. These studies are of interest because they contain the first mention of such characteristic Hegelian concepts as *Aufhebung* (a process of simultaneous dissolution and preservation in a broader perspective, usually translated as "transcendence" or "sublation"), dialectical progress, and *Versöhnung* (reconciliation). Christianity developed, according to Hegel, from Catholicism, through Protestantism, to philosophy, from the witnessing of revelation to ascertainment and intellectual knowledge. The mediation of philosophy will bring about a higher form of religion through the "sublation" and reconciliation of opposites. This mediation is to be conceived of in such a way that the new idea absorbs the whole of life, doing justice to all finite opposites and contradictions by means of *Aufhebung* in a threefold sense: by abolishing and yet simultaneously preserving them and by raising them to a living coherence in some higher absorption.

The so-called *Fragment of a System of Frankfurt* (dated September 14, 1800), while not yet constituting a system, does sketch out the framework of one. It lacks, however, the poetic ardor and vitality of Hölderlin's style. The long, refractory sentences testify to laborious thinking. Though this early work does not present the dialectical method in detail, Hegel thinks in terms of dialectics and historical development and sees a union, reconciliation, and sublation as their ultimate destiny.[31] The closing lines of this rough draft anticipate Hegel's later writings on the role of the individual in history:

"Every individual is a blind link in the chain of absolute necessity, along which the world develops. Every individual can raise himself to domination over a great length of this chain only if he realizes the goal of this great necessity and, by virtue of this knowledge, learns to speak the magic words which evoke its shape. The knowledge of how to simultaneously absorb and elevate oneself beyond the total energy of suffering and antithesis that has dominated the world and all forms of its development for thousands of years—this knowledge can be gathered from philosophy alone."[32]

We should not overlook the fact that even in the early so-called theological writings, Hegel dealt extensively with problems of political philosophy. His political interest, which had never died, reawakened in Frankfurt. "Leaving his parental home, the home of an official, Hegel had moved from a capital city to an idyllic university town; now, he was changing over from a patriarchal family aristocracy in Berne to the city of a mercantile, moneyed aristocracy."[33] Hegel made synopses of articles from English newspapers in order to familiarize himself with "conditions of profit and property" in England; he kept abreast of parliamentary speeches on the "poor taxes" and the reform of common law in Prussia, and severely criticized the penal code.

Rosenkranz writes that, starting in August 1798, Hegel devoted himself to a thorough investigation of Kant's moral and legal philosophy as well as *The Metaphysics of Ethics*. "He wanted to comprehend, to discuss it through and through. . . . He strove . . . to unite the legality of positive law and the morality of subjectivity (that knows itself to be good or evil) in a higher concept, which, in these commentaries, he often simply referred to as 'life,' but later called 'ethics.' He protested against the dismemberment of man in the casuistics resulting from the despotism of a sense of duty."[34] Hegel attacked primarily Kant's conception of the relationship between State and Church, which Kant expressed in the following terms:

"The two of them, Church and State, ought to leave each other alone; they have no business interfering with one another."

Hegel, on the contrary, wonders how and to what extent such a dichotomy is possible; he develops his definition of the two institutions from the principle of totality and characteristically concludes that "a human being must not be split into a discrete political and a discrete religious being," and that "Church and State cannot be separated."

The Death of Hegel's Father

In the midst of these studies, his sister sent him a letter dated January 5, 1799: "Yesterday just before midnight, our father died calmly and peacefully. I am unable to write any more. God help me! Your Christiane."[35]

Hegel left for Stuttgart on March 9 to settle the estate. His mother having died fifteen years earlier, the legacy was divided among the children. He returned to Frankfurt on May 28, 1799, with his share—3,154 florins, 24 kreutzers, and 4 pfennigs. Possessed of this minor fortune, to which he added his savings, Hegel was now able to give up his tutoring and prepare for an academic career.

(4)

The Years in Jena

Privatdozent and Professor of Philosophy
In those days, Jena was the capital of German philosophy, and
Weimar the capital of German literature. At the turn of the cen-
tury, the University of Jena had such teachers as Schiller, Fichte,
the Schlegel brothers (August Wilhelm and Friedrich), Fries, Krause,
Schad, and Schelling.

Goethe had been instrumental in getting the University to offer the
twenty-three-year-old Schelling a teaching position in 1798. The
correspondence between Schelling and Hegel had fallen off since
1795; imperceptibly, their relationship had altered slightly, and
Hegel was very aware of it. But Schelling was now the only person
who could do anything for him. So, on November 2, 1800, Hegel
wrote from Frankfurt:

"I think, dear Schelling, that despite several years of separation,
I need not feel embarrassed about appealing to your good nature
in regard to a particular wish of mine. My request is for a few
addresses in Bamberg, where I wish to stay a while. Now that I
am finally able to leave my present position, I am determined to
remain independent for some time and devote myself to papers
and studies I have begun working on. Before giving myself over to
the wild literary life of Jena, I first want to fortify myself in· another place. I thought of Bamberg, especially because I hoped to
meet you there; I hear that you're back in Jena, and I don't know
a living soul in Bamberg, nor do I know where else I might get

some addresses. . . . I'm looking for cheap food, a stout beer for my physical well-being, and a few acquaintances; all things being equal, I would prefer a Catholic city to a Protestant one; I want to see the former religion from up close for once. . . .

"I have followed your great public career with admiration and joy. You will excuse me from either talking about that with humility and also from wanting to prove myself to you. I shall use the intermediary of words, hoping that we shall find each other again as friends. In my scholarly education, which started with the more subordinate needs of man, I had to be driven to scholarliness, and my adolescent ideal had to transform itself simultaneously into a form of reflection and a system. I now wonder—as long as I am still occupied with the problem—what return to an involvement in the life of people can be found. Of all the people I view about me, I see you as the only person in whom, with regard to expression and influence on the world, I would like to find my friend; for I realize that you have grasped man purely, that is, with your entire mind, heart, and soul, and without vanity. This is why, in regard to myself, I feel such great confidence that you will recognize my selfless striving (even if its sphere were lower) and discover some value in it."[36]

Schelling told his friend to come directly to Jena and live at his place for the time being. In early 1801, Hegel accepted the invitation and got right to work. During the next six years of his new activity, he brought out at an amazing speed—considering his former slow, deliberate ways—a series of longer and briefer writings which were to establish his reputation. "Completely unknown to the literary world at a fairly mature age, he suddenly entered a crowd in which literary activity was universal; he therefore had to at least roughly mark out the position he wanted to occupy."[37]

In a few short months, he wrote his first philosophical work: *Difference Between Fichte's and Schelling's Systems of Philosophy.* The book was occasioned by Karl Leonhard Reinhold, who, glossing over the dissimilarities between the two systems, posited their total identity. Hegel, while allowing Fichte's philosophy to be "an immortal masterpiece of speculation," felt that it did not suffice as a system, because Fichte attained "neither a concept of nature nor a concept of ethics or aesthetic culture and civilization." And although enthusiastically approving of Schelling's philosophy of nature and of the mind, Hegel cautiously pointed out the shortcomings and juxtaposed his own philosophical point of view.

At the end of the summer semester, Hegel submitted to the faculty a dissertation in German, together with a shortened Latin translation, *De orbitis planetarum;* this was mainly a critique of Kepler's

Friedrich Wilhelm Joseph von Schelling (drawing by G. Klotz).

and Newton's scientific method. On his thirty-first birthday, August 27, 1801, the qualifying examination took place, and Hegel received his *venia legendi* (the right to lecture at a German university).

In the winter semester of 1801–1802, Hegel became a *Privatdozent* (unsalaried lecturer) with an average of twenty to thirty students. He gave one public and one private lecture series for a fee of "three French crownpieces." Each series took four hours a week. In the first semester, he dealt with *Logic and Metaphysics* and had an audience of only eleven; later, he lectured on *Natural Law ex dictatis,* as well as mathematics. For the summer semester of 1803, he announced that he would present all philosophy as a system and during the winter semesters of 1803–1804 and 1804–1805 he repeatedly referred to his *Primer of the Philosophical Encyclopedia,* which was supposedly coming out in the next few weeks or during the current semester, but never did. Hegel's lectures on the *History of Philosophy* (1805) were extraordinary. They show that from the very first, he included the historical development of philosophical consciousness as a decisive factor in his nascent system.

Hegel did not have an easy time gaining acceptance. Twelve other teachers, six of them *Privatdozenten,* were lecturing on philosophy. Schelling was apparently overpowering at that time. "He combined self-assurance with rhetorical facility. Moreover, his audience was fascinated by his aura of being a revolutionary in philosophy, an aura that Schelling always created around his ingeniously careless, aristocratically indefinable person. . . . Hegel's simple ways formed a sharp contrast to this. His presentation was that of a man who, totally forgetting himself and concentrating on the subject matter, was never at a loss for the appropriate phrase, but did lack oratorical richness. . . . Relentlessly opposed to rhetorical elegance, always speaking to the point . . . Hegel succeeded in captivating his students with the intensity of his speculation. His voice resembled his eyes. These were large but introverted, the refracted gaze filled with deep ideality, which at certain moments would exert a visible and poignant power. His voice was rather ample but not sonorous; it was only because of its apparent ordinariness that the inspiration came through, creating the power of knowledge, and in the moments when the genius of mankind reached the audience through that voice, no one was left unmoved. The earnestness in his noble features at first had something that, although not intimidating, kept others at a distance; but the gentleness and amiability of his expression were winning and inviting. A peculiar smile revealed pure kindness, yet with a touch of asperity, even sarcasm, sadness, or perhaps irony."[38]

During the summer semester of 1806, Hegel taught every afternoon from three to four and from five to six. Once, napping after lunch, he suddenly awoke, heard a clock strike, and thought it was time for his course. He dashed to the lecture hall, where students were waiting for Augusti, a professor of theology, who taught there from two to three. Hegel commenced his lecture and was so engrossed that he failed to notice a student who was trying to call his attention to the time. Meanwhile, Augusti arrived at the door and heard someone lecturing; recognizing Hegel's voice and assuming that he himself had come an hour late, Augusti left. At three o'clock, Hegel's students, who had been informed of the mix-up, assembled, and Hegel began his lecture with the words: "Gentlemen, of the experiences of self-awareness, the first is that of the truth or rather untruth of sensory certainty. This is where we stopped, and an hour ago I myself had a very special experience of this nature."[39]

Hegel's gregariousness brought him many friends in Jena; he was a bright conversationalist and a welcome guest in the homes of Frommann, Knebel, and Seebeck. In addition, he seems to have often received company in his own place. He bought wine from the Ramann Brothers in Erfurt, and his orders were a part of his regular correspondence. Thus, in July 1802, he wrote: "May I request another fourteen-gallon measure of *Pontak,* but please dispatch it as soon as possible so that it may be shipped by night, since at the present time it might come to harm during the day. And please send me a good quality, as I find wines of yours coming here at the same prices as, but of a better quality than, the ones I receive. I feel that in view of my consumption and the punctuality of my payment, I merit equally good wine; with this hope I therefore request one fourteen-gallon measure @ twenty-six thalers."[40]

Besides Schelling, other Swabians resided in Jena, the most important one being Friedrich Immanuel Niethammer. A native of Beilstein, he was probably Hegel's most loyal and helpful friend. He taught philosophy, and, together with Fichte, had edited the *Philosophisches Journal,* which had printed the articles that had led to the attacks on Fichte for "atheism." In 1803, Niethammer joined the Bavarian civil service and moved to Würzburg, becoming professor in the "Department of Knowledge Necessary for the Education of Religious Instructors in Elementary Schools" (as the theological faculty was called for a while in the jargon of the reorganized University). Subsequently, he became an administrative councilor in Bamberg, and was honored with a high position on the central school board in Munich.

After the atheism controversy and Fichte's dismissal, a furtive discontent stole from mind to mind, according to Goethe. Schlegel and Tieck had left Jena, Novalis had died, Schiller had settled in Weimar, Fichte had moved to Berlin; Hufeland, Paulus, and Schelling accepted teaching posts at the University of Würzburg in 1803. With Schelling gone, he and Hegel had to terminate their joint work on the *Critical Journal of Philosophy,* which they had founded in 1802. Schelling had edited a new *Periodical for Speculative Physics* at the same time so that the *Journal* was almost solely Hegel's work. In fact, most of the articles were written by him, including *On the Essence of Philosophical Criticism.* In this essay, Hegel took a stand against the delusion of those who establish different philosophies side by side and forget that all philosophy is one. He also opposed the striving for originality of thought and the degeneration of speculative thinking through erroneous popularizing. Next to writings of a political nature, the disquisition on *Faith and Knowledge or The Reflective Philosophy of Subjectivity* must be emphasized because of its penetrating, if unilateral, critique of the philosophy of Kant, Fichte, and Jacobi. Hegel feels that in the "reflective philosophy" advocated by these three men, reason "is only directed at the empirical," and that these philosophers, in struggling against the finite have merely remained within its immediate sphere:

"Kant's [philosophy] and Fichte's have achieved the level of Notion [*Begriff*] but not that of pure Idea [*Idee*] . . . thus, the goal of such philosophy can only be, not to know God, but what is called Man. Man and mankind are their absolute point of view: that is, as a fixed, insurmountable finitude of reason, not as the reflection of eternal beauty, the mental focus of the universe, but as an absolute materiality, which, however, is able to believe that it can daub itself here and there with an alien metaphysics. As if art, limited to portraiture, sought its ideal by adding a touch of yearning to the eye of an ordinary face, or a melancholy smile to the mouth, yet were forbidden to depict the gods, who are beyond yearning and melancholy (as if the representation of eternal images were possible only at the expense of the human); thus, philosophy should depict not the Idea of Man, but the abstraction of empirical mankind mixed with limitation, and [it should] carry the deep, rigid thorn of absolute contrast, and by making plain its restriction to the Material (it can analyze this abstraction or else completely refrain from it in the pathetic manner of aesthetes) it can simultaneously adorn itself with the superficial paint of metaphysics by referring us on with faith in something higher.

But truth cannot be duped by such sanctity of finitude, which abides: for true sanctification would have to destroy it."[41]

Meanwhile, Hegel was attracting attention. In the year 1804, he was unanimously appointed to the position of "assessor" at the *Mineralogical Society* of Jena, and he became a fellow of the *Westphalian Society for Natural Research.* Three years later, he was elected honorary member of the *Physics Society of Heidelberg.* When, toward the end of 1803, it occurred to the administration to make Fries *professor extraordinarius* [roughly the equivalent of an American professor], Hegel wrote to Goethe at the Ministry of Weimar on February 24, 1804:

"Having heard that several of my colleagues are awaiting their gracious appointment as Professors of philosophy, I am reminded that I am the oldest of the lecturers in philosophy here; therefore I beg Your Excellency to allow me to inquire whether I must not fear being restricted in working to the best of my abilities at the university because of such an adjustment on the part of the highest authorities. . . . I know full well that this matter requires the gracious approval of Your Excellency . . . at the same time [I know] how much my efforts were fired by the thought that the Most Serene Protectors would at least be graciously considerate enough not to think me inferior to others."[42]

Exactly one year later, Hegel became an associate professor, and the following year he was granted an annual salary of 100 thalers, the news of which came from Goethe in a cordially worded letter. The payment was disappointingly small, but the treasury of Weimar was depleted. Goethe wrote: "Please regard this, my dear Doctor Hegel, at least as proof that I have not stopped working privately on your behalf. I most certainly would rather have more to tell you; but in such cases, a great deal can be gained for the future once a start has been made."[43]

The Phenomenology of Mind

In the winter of 1805, Hegel decided to go ahead with the publication of a work that had been planned and promised for so long. The book was to be printed by the bookdealer Goebhardt in Bamberg, and the first part was to contain an introduction called *The Phenomenology of Mind*. This work forms the high point of Hegel's philosophical development. All the later writings, apart from their individual significance, are basically no more than a careful exposition, with a tighter structure and a deeper exploration, of the ideas set forth in *The Phenomenology of Mind.*[44]

Hegel was to get approximately one gulden a page, and the first payment was due after the printing of half the book. But when is a work in progress "half" completed? Kant had made it a rule never to send a manuscript to the printer until the final period had been put down. When Hegel delayed after sending 384 pages, the publisher reduced the stipulated number of one thousand copies to 750 and refused to pay Hegel anything until he received the finished manuscript. Hegel, in great financial straits, asked his friend Niethammer in Bamberg for help. Niethammer in turn promised the publisher that he would buy up the entire edition at 12 gulden per copy if Hegel did not deliver the manuscript by October 18, 1806. On the basis of this generous guarantee, the publisher paid Hegel for the 384 pages. Hegel thanked his friend in a letter dated October 8, 1806:

"How glad I am that you have straightened out this whole complicated business, and how greatly indebted to you I am! . . . I could explain the extent of my gratitude only by describing how perplexed I was by the matter. Let us hope that it will be completed as felicitously. The first half of the manuscript is enclosed; you will receive the second half on Friday, and then I shall have done everything expected of me. If any part were to be lost, I would be at my wits' end; it would be very difficult to write it over again, and the book could not come out this year."[45]

The Battle of Jena

Hegel's concern over a possible loss of the manuscript was not unfounded. Napoleon was standing before the very walls of Jena. On October 13, 1806, the city was taken, and "on the day that

Friedrich Immanuel Niet-hammer (silhouette).

Jena was occupied by the French, and Emperor Napoleon arrived within its walls," Hegel wrote these famous lines to Niethammer, evincing his admiration of "world-historic personalities":

"I saw the Emperor—that world-soul—riding out to reconnoiter the city; it is truly a wonderful sensation to see such an individual, concentrated here on a single point, astride a single horse, yet reaching across the world and ruling it. . . . To make such progress from Thursday to Monday is possible only for this extraordinary man, whom it is impossible not to admire."[46]

The soldiers began plundering, and Hegel had to put up with their onslaught in his home. He was threatened by more serious unpleasantness, when, suddenly noticing the Cross of the French Legion of Honor on a corporal's coat, he told the officer that he hoped that a man honored by such insignia would treat even a simple German scholar honorably. Thereupon the looters quieted down and settled for a few bottles of wine. But eventually Hegel did have to flee; pocketing the final pages destined for Bamberg and leaving everything else to its fate, he sought refuge in an empty student room at the University Vice-president's house, where a high-ranking officer was billeted. Later, when Hegel was able to go home, he discovered that "those fellows had churned my papers around like lottery tickets." He couldn't even find a pen and paper to write a letter.

Once again, Hegel was under severe financial pressure. Goethe, much concerned, wrote to his friends in Jena, including "Herr Professor Hegel in the Old Fencing-Hall," and instructed Knebel to give the philosopher "up to ten thalers." On October 20, Hegel managed to send off the rest of the manuscript, which—as historians have ever since dramatically described it—he "brought to completion amidst the thunder of the Battle of Jena." Hegel's pecuniary situation was forcing him to make some sort of decision. His tiny capital had been consumed long before; his income from writing and teaching and his annual stipend were too small to sustain him. The university was in a period of decline, and Hegel, weary of the provisional state of things, tired of leading the life of a boarder, and yearning for some sort of change, once more appealed to Schelling, who had accepted a respectable offer at the University of Munich:

"For some time, I had been hopefully glancing here and there; however, it still seems to be generally assumed that just about anybody can teach philosophy—or rather, since people are aware that neither scholarship nor any faculty can exist without philosophy, and since they feel at the same time that the two contain nothing philosophical and yet have come a long way without it— they seem to think that philosophy consists in this 'nothing'. . . . Being closer to the source, you may know more precisely what plans they have [in Munich] and you can simultaneously judge whether any prospects exist for me there; if so, please let me call upon your friendship for news, advice, and even help. I would be highly desirous of finding a situation that was outwardly somewhat secure." [47]

Schelling assured him by return mail of his "unswerving and profound friendship." He knew that a philosopher was needed in Landshut (what would later become the University of Munich had moved there from Ingolstadt). He regretted, however, that he "could not even try to speak on behalf of his friend," but advised him to send the minister, Count Mortgelas, a copy of the work that was to appear at Easter 1807. "What will be created, if your maturity takes some more time to ripen its fruits! I can only wish you quiet and leisure for the execution of such substantial and, as it were, timeless works." [48]

Editing the Bamberger Zeitung

In the nick of time, Hegel received an offer from Niethammer to edit the *Bamberger Zeitung*. This was not quite what Hegel was hoping for, but now he had still another reason for finding a steady source of income. On February 5, 1807, his landlord's wife in Jena bore him an illegitimate son, of whom more shall be said later on. Consequently, on February 20, 1807, he promptly replied that he had decided to accept the position. "The work itself will interest me, since, as you know, I like to keep abreast of international events." He stipulated only "that the nature of this employment will not require any commitment on my part with regard to time; you yourself recently indicated this. I cannot be totally without the hope of a formal offer from Heidelberg or at least that a periodical may be founded there and that I be asked to edit it. I myself as well as my work would undoubtedly profit more from that than from editing the *Bamberger Zeitung*—not to mention the connection I would thus have with the university."[49]

For the time being, the offer from Heidelberg did not come. Until Easter 1808, Hegel was to all intents and purposes a professor on leave from the University of Jena, which continued paying his salary. When the newspaper's finances were set in order, he was able to get along in Bamberg on over 1300 gulden annually. But soon he was groaning under the "newspaper yoke," felt like a newspaper galley-slave, and worst of all, chafed under Bavarian censorship. Within a few weeks he wrote to Niethammer (who meanwhile had become a senior inspector of schools and an influential member of the "Department of Institutions of Instruction and Education"): "This work cannot be considered a solid establishment." Once again, his friend helped him with a recommendation. "How would you feel," he asked, in a letter accompanying a "culinary present" from his wife, "about being suggested for the position of headmaster in a *Gymnasium*?"[50]

5

The Headmaster in Nuremberg

In 1808, Niethammer drew up a school-reform plan, "General Norma-
tive for Organizing the Public Institutions of Learning," which put
the Bavarian school system in order at last. The basis of the secondary school *(Gymnasium)* remained the study of ancient languages
and literature. In the four higher classes, the students were to be
initiated into philosophy; in the humanistic institutions, this meant
"the speculative study of ideas"; in the science-oriented *Realgym-
nasium,* "the contemplative study of ideas." A headmaster should, if
at all possible, be a philosopher and teach both philosophy and
religion.

Niethammer was afraid that Hegel might consider the offer of
a position as headmaster at the Nuremberg *Gymnasium* an insulting
degradation. However, after his Bamberg interim, Hegel was extremely happy about the prospect of regular and respectable work
"whose duties would re-establish his contact with scholarship."

Hegel as a Teacher

On November 15, 1808, the appointment was made: "In the
name of His Majesty of Bavaria, Through Utmost Respect, on the
fourteenth of November, His Royal Majesty of Bavaria has most
graciously appointed Professor Hegel of Bamberg headmaster of the
Gymnasium here in Nuremberg and professor of preparatory philosophy
at the same. He has therefore to assume his new official duties immediately following the forthcoming instructions from the district

board of education. Royal General Commission of the Pegnitz District. Thürheim."[51]

Hegel's job at the Ägidien-*Gymnasium* brought him a good deal of trouble. As a professor, he received only 900 gulden annually, and as a headmaster 100 gulden plus free lodging, which the administrator tried to interpret as meaning 100 gulden *or* free lodging. Hegel complained to Niethammer, writing: "In this case, I must admit I would gladly relinquish the headmaster's job to anyone else."[52] The financial situation was so disorderly that the salary was always paid late, and Hegel occasionally found himself unable to take care of his daily living expenses. There was no school-attendant, no copyist, no reimbursement for stationery, and the school bookshop sold textbooks at higher prices than any private store. Hegel finally succeeded in procuring money to whitewash the *Gymnasium* rooms but not his official residence; the walls hadn't been whitewashed for fifty years. Conditions were so appalling that neither the Ägidien-*Gymnasium,* the Sebaldus-*Schule,* nor the Lorenz-*Schule* had toilets, and the pupils were forced to go to private homes nearby.

Pedagogically, Hegel was a great success; after all, having been a private tutor for eight years, he was no stranger to teaching. Rosenkranz is correct in stating that it is easy to say "the speculative Pegasus was harnessed by force of necessity to a *Gymnasium* cart and, for lack of a university auditorium, Hegel had to content himself with secondary school pupils." It is true that he viewed his job as something temporary, hoping all the while for a professorship in Tübingen, then Heidelberg, then Berlin, and for an expression of interest from Holland. Yet, as his letters indicate, for the time being he was happy and inwardly gratified to devote himself to his duties. After all, it was explicitly stipulated that as headmaster he would also be teaching philosophy. Hegel was far from being the sort of arrogant genius who considers himself too good to bother with the less complex mind of a young person. On the contrary, one has the impression that Hegel achieved greater clarity by teaching high school, pedagogically disciplining and suppressing the romantic extravagance and the pseudomystical tinge that were not exactly alien to him. Thus, one result of these *Gymnasium* years was his growing conviction that philosophy is teachable; a second consequence was his use of original philosophical terminology.[53]

In 1816, while re-applying for a position at the University of Jena, Hegel wrote to Frommann: "My first attempt at lecturing there gave rise, as I have since discovered, to a prejudice against me. I was a beginner; I hadn't yet worked my way to clarity; and when speaking I was tied to the words in my notebook. Now,

Hegel (engraving by Bollinger, based on Xeller's portrait).

nearly eight years of practice at the *Gymnasium,* where the basic requirement in the constant reciprocity of discussion is to be intelligible and therefore as clear as possible, have brought me total freedom."

Apart from that, Hegel was of the opinion that philosophy should not be taught at a secondary school; first, because the later university students, feeling that they have philosophized more than enough in *Gymnasium,* think they can do justice to philosophy by simply taking a course or two; and then because many high school instructors lack philosophical training, and their teaching often arouses more aversion than interest.

Hegel's occasionally robust, almost visual articulateness made his classes quite lively. Citing examples of "pathological delusion," Hegel explained: One man assumes "that when he pisses he is flooding an entire city; another believes he is a grain of barley about to be eaten by chickens; a third one thinks he has glass feet, a little bell in his body, etc."[54] Anyone imagining that Hegel especially prepared a concrete philosophy for school use will be surprised by the following statements in his Official Report on the Teaching of Philosophy (1812):

"In the teaching of philosophy at secondary schools, the main thing is *abstract form.* The young pupils must lose their eyesight and their hearing, they must be diverted from thinking concretely, be withdrawn into the inner night of the soul; on this basis they must learn to see, to retain definitions, and to make specific differentiations. Furthermore, *abstract thinking* is learned only by thinking abstractly. One can start with the sensible and the concrete and then work one's way analytically to the abstract, thereby—as it seems—going the *natural* way, that is, from easier to more difficult things. Or else, one can begin immediately with the abstract, taking it per se, teaching and making it understandable. *First of all:* concerning a comparison of both methods, the former is no doubt *more natural* and therefore *unscholarly and unscientific.* . . . *Secondly:* it is entirely erroneous to regard the natural way, which begins with the *concrete and sensible* and leads to thinking, as the *easier* method. Quite the reverse is true: that method is more difficult, just as it is easier to pronounce and read individual letters—the elements of spoken language—than whole words. The abstract, being simpler, is easier to grasp. The concrete, sensible paraphernalia have to be stripped off anyway; it is therefore superfluous to include them in the first place, since they have to be disposed of, and thus they merely distract."[55]

Hegel would teach by dictating a paragraph and then interpreting it. Although he lectured without reading notes, he would have prepared manuscripts lying before him, and looked straight ahead, spilling snuff right and left. The students had to prepare clean drafts of the dictation. (The original notebooks and these copies formed the basis of Rosenkranz's edition of *The Philosophical Propaedeutics,* which included the speeches Hegel made as headmaster.) From time to time, Hegel would call upon some pupil to read his final draft out loud, and at the beginning of every lesson one of them would have to orally sum up the previous lecture. Anyone could ask him a question, even interrupt him; good-natured as Hegel was, he occasionally spent the better part of the lesson "supplying information."

But for all his leniency and friendliness, his authority was indisputable. The pupils, whom in the higher grades he addressed as *Herr* (Mister), had to overcome a certain aloofness on his part in order to approach him. Hegel's having taught philosophy at the university, as well as his being a well-known author and the associate of many famous men, impressed the students enormously. "But the profound earnestness persistently manifest in everything Hegel said and did, his aura of matter-of-fact gravity, commanded great respect from his students. If another teacher fell ill, Hegel would often take over for him and without further ado conduct a class in Greek or German literature, integral and differential calculus. If a pupil wished to delve more deeply into philosophy, Hegel would refer him to Plato and Kant, never failing to warn him that reading the popular philosophers was a waste of time. He had the seniors come to him, so that he might paternally discuss their future with them and give them helpful tips for their university studies." However, one of his earlier pupils told Hegel's biographer Rosenkranz that the headmaster heaped severe censure on "all student games" and—while taking hearty doses of snuff himself—declaimed against the disgraceful vice of smoking.[56]

Marriage to Marie von Tucher

Meanwhile, Hegel had turned forty, and there were no signs of his marrying. His philosophical profession was the very substance of his life. Like Moses, he suffered from a speech impediment and was wont to say that God had condemned him to be a philosopher. Intellectual uneasiness made him doubt whether he was meant to lead a happy life on earth, let alone to make a woman happy in marriage. In point of fact, a constant involvement with the problems of the world and man does not exactly make one fit for a middle-class life of ease. Love of wisdom requires absolute truthfulness; yet truth has to be found by critical examination; the slightest shift of emphasis will lead to error. A critical attitude of this kind will force the philosopher off the naive or normal path and might even make him unbearable to other people. Until the decline of the middle ages, philosophers were almost always priests or monks and hence celibate; but though not clerics, Descartes, Malebranche, Spinoza, Leibniz, Wolff, Locke, Hume, and Kant, too, remained bachelors. However, Fichte had a wife, Schelling followed suit by marrying Caroline Schlegel, and now Hegel was about to join the ranks of married men.

From a letter dated April 18, 1811, Niethammer was the first to learn the surprising news:

"I hear that if you remain you will be able to do more for the university than in your work hitherto. Since the matter is still unsettled this letter of mine might be doubly superfluous. But a more immediate instigation for it exists—matrimony with a dear, dear, good girl. My happiness is partly dependent on my obtaining a position at the university. The day before yesterday, I received the assurance that I can call this dear heart mine—I know you wish me the very best of luck. I therefore told her I would write to you and your excellent wife first. Her name is—Marie von Tucher."[57]

Marie was the daughter of the Senator from the imperial city of Nuremberg, Jobst Wilhelm Karl Baron Tucher von Simmelsdorf; her mother was Susanna née Baroness Haller von Hallerstein. The bride-to-be, the eldest of seven children, had just turned twenty. The engagement apparently took place in April; but we know nothing of the time preceding it. Hegel extolled his young fiancee in enthusiastic poems:

> You are mine! I may call such a heart mine,
>   Recognizing in your gaze
> The reflection of love,
>   O bliss, O supreme happiness!
>
> How I love you, now I can say it;
>   Everything in my constricted heart
> Which secretly beat for you so long,
>   I can allow to become audible desire!
>
> But poor word, love's delight,
>   What surges and drives inside myself
> Into the heart, cannot be expressed
>   By your limited strength.
>
> I could, nightingale, envy
>   The power of your throat,
> But malevolent nature has made
>   Only the language of suffering so eloquent!
>
> But though denying the lips
>   The words to express love's bliss,
> Nature did lend them
>   A more fervent sign
>
> Of the union of lovers;
>   The kiss is profounder language,
> In which souls meet,
>   And my heart flows into yours. [58]

For all this, Hegel did have qualms about his fitness for conjugal bliss. In a letter Marie wrote to his sister, he added a few lines which deeply hurt his fiancée:

"After setting down these words that are before me and whose meaning is so dear to me: 'Can you tell how happy I can be with her for the rest of my life, and how happy I am now for having gained a love I had stopped aspiring to in this world?'—I added, almost as if my feeling of happiness and my expression of it had been too great compared with what we had spoken: 'insofar as

Marie Hegel in later years.

happiness lies within the destiny of my life.' I don't think that this should have hurt your feelings! You must remember, dear Marie, that your deeper thoughts, the formation of the spiritual in you, have taught you, too, that in profound natures any feeling of happiness is joined by a feeling of melancholy. And also remember that you promised to be my healer for any remaining lack of faith in contentment, that is, to reconcile my true feelings with my—all too frequent—way of being both against and for reality; that this aspect gives your destiny a loftier side; that I believe you capable of the necessary strength; that this strength must lie in *our* love." [59]

Marie's family was worried about the irregular income of the couple, for besides the dowry, the bride would receive only 100 gulden yearly. Consequently, the wedding was to take place only when Hegel would go back to teaching at a university. Once again, Niethammer came to the rescue; in a letter to Hegel, which was obviously meant to be shown t. the Tucher family, he wrote that an offer from the University of Erlangen was as good as certain. Besides, as a professor and as headmaster of one of the most respected royal secondary schools, Hegel could consider himself worthy enough. After all, personal merit and a position acquired by his own efforts nowadays endowed a man with more nobility than any number of ancestors. Niethammer said that futile anxieties were ill-becoming to a philosopher and ought not to stop Hegel from having the ceremony as soon as possible.[60]

Hegel's Sons

On September 16, 1811, the 41-year-old philosopher and the 20-year-old girl were joined in a marriage that was to endure in serene happiness and mutual love until Hegel's death in 1831. Their first child, a daughter, died soon after her birth. Next came two sons: the elder, named Karl after his grandfather, became a professor of history at the University of Erlangen and died at the age of eighty-five; the younger, christened Immanuel after his godfather Niethammer, became the Consistorial President of the Province of Brandenburg and lived until the age of 77.

Hegel's eldest son was actually the illegitimate child previously mentioned, who was christened Ludwig; for a long time, more guesswork existed about him than known facts. Even now, after Georg Lasson's publication of all discoverable sources, different versions obtain concerning Hegel's relationship to his first-born. They are based on either the boy's letters of complaint about his father or statements by the diplomat and writer, Varnhagen.

According to Varnhagen, the following had happened: Hegel had an affair in Jena with his landlord's wife, Christiana Charlotte Burkhardt, née Fischer. On February 5, 1807, she bore a third illegitimate child, the aforenamed Ludwig. The parish register of Jena lists as godfathers: Friedrich Frommann, the publisher, and Hegel's brother, Lieutenant Georg Ludwig Hegel. Shortly thereafter, when Frau Burkhardt's husband died, Hegel supposedly told the widow he would marry her, only to forget his promise when he left Jena. But after his marriage to Marie von Tucher, Ludwig's mother turned up and "in the vilest and most sordid fashion" demanded some kind of settlement. Hegel's wife, upon being fully informed of the matter, showed great faith in her love and took the child into the house. As the boy grew up, he suffered from the drawback inherent in his very presence and became withdrawn, timid, and cunning. Finally, Hegel decided to apprentice him to a merchant in Stuttgart. The boy embezzled the insignificant sum of 8 groschen, but the theft brought matters to a head and gave Hegel a sufficient pretext for declaring him "unworthy." From then on, he was required to bear the name of Fischer, which he suffered as a mortal indignity. Hegel bought him a commission in the Colonial Army of the Netherlands. According to the records of the

Dutch-East Indian military headquarters, Ludwig died in Djakarta on August 28, 1831, as the result of *"febris inflammatoria."* [61]

A perusal of Ludwig's letters reveals that he felt neglected by his stepmother, that he always feared rather than loved his parents, developed a great gift for languages at school and was even head of his class for a while in Greek and Latin, and that he wanted to study medicine but was bullied into his business apprenticeship. He claims that after an argument with his rather arbitrary master, he asked to be dismissed. He was unaware of any delinquency on his part other than being unsuited to a trade for which he felt no inclination whatsoever. Hegel—he no longer cared to call him "father"—hadn't written to say goodbye when the son entered the army and had even refused to send him his linen and his books. [62]

It is hard to ferret out the truth. But we *can* establish that Hegel always provided for the boy. He certainly never entirely disavowed him; otherwise Goethe could not possibly have shown interest for "little Hegel" in Jena, where he wrote the following verses in the 10-year-old's album:

> *I saw you as a little boy*
> *Braving the world with huge self-confidence;*
> *However the world may treat you in the future,*
> *Be of good hope, your friend's eyes will bless you.*

Hegel's refusal to take his son along to Bamberg or to Nuremburg should not necessarily be viewed as selfishness. Being a bachelor, Hegel had no way of providing steadily for the boy. As soon as he began teaching at Heidelberg, he took the child into his home and sent him to good schools. Marie Hegel's letters indicate that she took a great deal of trouble with the difficult boy and that she tried to mediate in his fights with his legitimate half-brothers. On the other hand, the entries in the budget book of 1819 show, for example, that very little was spent for Ludwig's twelfth birthday whereas the fifth birthday of Immanuel, the youngest, involved a considerable sum.

The Science of Logic

In the winter following the marriage, the first two parts of *The Science of Logic (Wissenschaft der Logik)* were completed. Relieved, Hegel wrote to Niethammer: "I hope to publish my book on logic next Easter; my psychology will come along later. . . . By autumn, my work for my lectures will have acquired a more popular and more affable form and be more suitable to the tone of a general textbook and of high school instruction, for I feel more affable every year, and entirely so this year now that I'm a married man."[63] In point of fact, the *Logic* had not been popularized into a "general textbook." It is actually one of the most difficult of philosophical works, and Hegel knew this only too well. A few months later he wrote to Niethammer again:

"144 pages of my *Logic* have been printed. By Easter, as many as 320 are to follow. What can I say for now, but that 400 to 500 pages constitute only the *first* part, that they do not yet contain anything of what is usually called logic, that they are metaphysical logic: the first book is on being, the second on essence, if indeed the second can still be included in part I. I'm up to my ears in it now. It is no small task to write a 500-page book of highly abstruse contents during the first semester of one's marriage. But *injuria temporum!* I'm no academic; achieving a suitable form would have taken me another year, and I need money to live on."[64]

Thus, the fact that Hegel's second major work, *The Science of Logic,* in three volumes, never assumed an easily readable form was connected to some degree with the circumstance that for six months Headmaster Hegel had received no salary. But then again, the material itself is extremely difficult. The *Logic* was "to terminate the unseemly spectacle of a cultured nation without a metaphysics, like a richly decorated temple without a high altar."

Logic, for Hegel, was not the same as logic in the conventional sense. He himself once said that in his logic he had developed "God's thoughts prior to creation." Logic, as Aristotle had conceived of it—that is, the doctrine of the forms and laws of thinking in concepts, judgments, and conclusions—makes up only a portion of Hegel's *Logik.* As a whole, it examines not forms or contents of human thinking, but the *Geist* spirit, the Idea in a purely non-spatial and timeless being-in-itself. Thus, concepts and logical propositions are essences rather than modes of thinking. The entire process of the world is taken as the self-development of Spirit, a process which can be presented in three stages. This process reveals the law of the dialectic and the essential structure of philosophy.

During the first stage, the World-Spirit *(Weltgeist)* is in a state of being-in-itself *(an-sich-sein)*; the corresponding philosophical discipline is *logic.* During the second phase, the World-Spirit reaches a state of *alienation, self-estrangement, otherness;* the alienation of the Spirit passes into nature, which is rooted in time and space; this condition is paralleled by the *philosophy of Nature.* At the third and highest level, the Spirit returns from self-estrangement to itself in a state of being-in-and-for-itself *(an-und-für-sich-sein),* corresponding to the *philosophy of the Spirit.*[65]

No sooner had the first part of the *Logic* appeared than Hegel

Hegel (chalk portrait by Friedrich Jügel).

heard critical comments from the neighboring city of Erlangen about the "inconceivable contradictions," particularly Hegel's belief in the identity of being and non-being. One of the most prominent detractors was the Swabian mathematician, Pfaff, an original, witty, and ingenious man, who with his dogged intelligence thoroughly analyzed the *Logic*. In his extremely humorous letters to Hegel, Pfaff confessed to being the sort whom the philosophers never convert. "Viewed mathematically, they are all wrong the moment they try to prove anything."

Three Offers of Professorships

In 1813, Hegel was promoted to school supervisor, which somewhat improved his poor financial condition. But his desire to return to university teaching had been steadily increasing. He wrote to Niethammer that he felt "like the Adam of the biblical play, who appears on stage early in the morning of the sixth day of creation, before the act of creation has been performed on him, and sings an aria beginning: 'Oh, if only I were created!'" [66]

Hegel heard that his name had been mentioned in reference to a position at the University of Tübingen. He also appealed to Church Councilor Paulus, who had been his predecessor in Nuremberg, to intercede on his behalf at the University of Heidelberg. Then there was an inquiry from Erlangen, asking Hegel to recommend someone for a position as professor of philosophy. In his eagerness to once more participate in some way in university life, Hegel entered his own name in the list of candidates, and the ministry actually went along with the suggestion. But as Hans Joachim Schoeps observes in his Centennial Report on Erlangen (*Das War Christian-Erlangen;* Erlangen, 1950, p. 55), the University's written offer was "framed in downright insultingly cool and business-like terms, since G. E. A. Mehmel [Professor of Philosophy and a Kantian] had made sure that the faculty fulfilled Munich's wish in the form of enduring obedience."

Then, in July and August 1816, two offers came almost simultaneously: a warm invitation to Heidelberg and a cautiously guarded one from Berlin. Vice-President Daub of the University of Heidelberg wrote:

"In a letter that I received from Karlsruhe yesterday, I was given an assignment gratifying both to myself and your friends here: namely, to ask you if you would be willing to accept a position as full professor of philosophy in our university. The annual salary is 1300 florins in cash, plus six cords of wheat and nine cords of chaff. I admit that this is little, but unfortunately I know that for the time being a greater sum cannot be voted. Thus, my hope for an affirmative answer to the above question would be very slight if I could not add, on the basis of my own and my colleague's long experience, that whenever professors have taught with some measure of zeal and gained some measure of approval, the Government has gradually given them considerable raises in salary and will continue to do so in the future. Now if you accepted this offer, Heidelberg would have a philosopher for the first time since the founding of the university (as you probably know, Spinoza was once approached, but to no avail). A philosopher brings zeal, and a philosopher named Hegel will bring a good deal more, of which certainly very few people here or elsewhere have any notion, and which cannot be acquired by zeal alone. As for approval, there shall be no lack of it, once they finally get a philosopher. My hopes, most honorable Sir, rest on this and on your magnanimity in the interest of scholarship and its revival (scholarship at German universities is petrified and fossilized). . . .

"If I can see the day that you join the University of Heidelberg, which I love like a foster-mother and will love until the end, a pure and invigorating ray of light will fall into my life." [67]

In Berlin, the second Chair of Philosophy (actually the first, since the second belonged to Solger) had become vacant through Fichte's death and had been unoccupied for two years. Friedrich von Raumer, the historian, had visited Hegel in Nuremberg and sent a report to Minister von Schuckmann and his colleagues in Berlin. Niebuhr, Link, and Solger championed Hegel, and they had gotten a list through the Berlin Senate on which Hegel's name stood at the top. But then, Dean de Wette sent a special note to Minister von Schuckmann, a Kantian and an opponent of Schelling's philosophy of nature. The dean claimed that Hegel was basically just a servile follower of Schelling, that Hegel's *Logic* was an obscure occultism, that when lecturing he was confused, nervous, ill-at-ease, and lacked clarity and fluency, and that it could hardly be assumed that Hegel had corrected these faults by teaching at a *Gymnasium*. The candidate Fries, on the other hand, was a philosopher of the Kantian school, and so forth. . . .

This explains the Minister's peculiar inquiry, which Hegel received on August 24, 1816:

"From a letter of Privy Counselor Niebuhr, the Ministry of the Interior has learned that you wish to be engaged at our university. The Chair of Philosophy is free; and in view of the reputation and esteem you have gained through your philosophical writings, the Ministry will be happy to consider you as a possible choice for this position. However, the Ministry does think that for the sake of the institution and your own sake as well, a certain qualm ought to be disposed of, and we shall state it frankly so that you as an honest man may examine it and comment on it. Since you have not given any academic lectures for a significant number of years, and since previously you had not taught very long academically, doubts have been raised from various quarters as to whether you are still fully possessed of the ability to give vivid and effective lectures in your field, which ability, as you yourself will agree, is so very necessary, because now, as the unfortunate goings-on in professional studies are becoming ubiquitously blatant, the minds of young men must be especially roused and led to this discipline [philosophy] by vigorous instruction. Relying on your understanding of the duties of a teacher of philosophy and the needs of scholarship, the Ministry leaves it up to you to determine whether you consider yourself sufficiently qualified for the obligations here, and we await your answer before taking any further action."[68]

Although the government bulletin of Bavaria had announced Hegel's appointment at Erlangen, and the University President had already congratulated him, Hegel no longer had any alternative: Heidelberg had to be chosen over Berlin and Erlangen.

6

Heidelberg

The difficulty of leaving Nuremberg was mitigated for Hegel by the fact that in Heidelberg he would be living near Paulus, Daub, and George Friedrich Creuzer. Because of the strain of packing, his wife had given birth prematurely, and so Hegel arrived in Heidelberg without her, on October 19, 1816. There, Eschenmayer, a fellow Swabian, and the Paulus family devoted themselves to him. This was the third time that the latter and Hegel lived in the same city. Frau Paulus, whose outspokenness and witty humor strongly appealed to Hegel, nursed him like a mother when he fell ill at one time; she sat at his bedside playing cards with him and discussing all sorts of matters. When the possibility of Hegel's transfer to Berlin came up, she did her best to dissuade him, jokingly asking him how he could live in a city where the people drank wine from thimbles. But because of differing political views, Hegel eventually had a falling-out with Paulus, and fifteen years of friendship came to an end.

In his inaugural lecture on October 28, 1816, Hegel referred to the pacification ensuing from Napoleon's exile to St. Helena and the Congress of Vienna:

"The World-Spirit was so busy with external reality that it could not turn inward and concentrate. Now that this torrent of reality has been stopped, the German nation has hewn its way out of the worst grossness and has salvaged its nationality, the basis of all living life: we may hope . . . that out of political interest and all other interests bound to common reality, scholarship, the free, rational world of the mind, will once more blossom forth. . . . The courage of truth, a faith in the power of the mind, is the prime requirement of philosophy. Man, being mind, may and should consider himself worthy of the Highest; he cannot esteem too greatly the stature and power of his mind; and if he retains this faith, nothing will be so hard and unyielding that it will not open up to him. The initially closed and concealed essence of the universe has no power that can resist the courage of cognition; it [the essence of the universe] must disclose itself to him, revealing its riches and its depths and giving them up to him for his enjoyment."[69]

The Encyclopedia of the Philosophical Sciences

Hegel was completely absorbed in the preparation of his lectures. Rather than dragging out the Jena manuscripts on logic, metaphysics, and political law, he lectured on aesthetics, anthropology, psychology, and—more frequently than before—history of philosophy. For the winter term of 1816–1817, he announced *The Encyclopedia of the Philosophical Sciences in Outline (Enzyklopädie der Philosophischen Wissenschaften im Grundíss)*, making use of his lecture notes from the Nuremberg *Gymnasìum;* as of the summer of 1817, the book appearing under this title formed the basis of his lectures.

Hegel gave two, and then three, courses, so that he taught a total of sixteen hours a week. The supply was generous, but there were few takers. Somewhat disappointed, he wrote to his wife:

". . . Yesterday I began my lectures, but the size of the audience was not as promising as we had been led to believe. I was, if not perplexed or impatient, at least astonished that our expectations had not been met. In one course, there were only four students. But Paulus consoled me by explaining that he, too, had lectured to only four or five. . . . After coming on the scene, one has to be content during the first half-year that one can at least appear in public. The students have to warm up to a teacher. . . ."[70]

As the semester wore on, he eventually had an audience of twenty at his *Encyclopedia* lecture and thirty in his course on the history of philosophy. Hegel was in a good frame of mind; he was very fond of the "quiet charming life" in a town distinguished for its natural beauty. He relished most of all the magnificent promenades; but his house in Friedrichstrasse also had a view of the hills and the chestnut forests. The students kept their distance; youthful timidity prevented them from speaking to him. But soon anecdotes began circulating about the strange, absent-minded stroller who, evidently forgetting everything around him, would often halt, presumably to cogitate about the World-Spirit, pure ideas, and Being. During the summer of 1817 (according to one story) he was walking lost in thought across the campus after a heavy rain had soaked the earth. One shoe remained stuck in the mud, but Hegel, not noticing it, ambled on in one stocking-foot. However, a Hegel cult, such as the one arising later in Berlin, did not develop; his two-year sojourn in Heidelberg was too short.

First Disciples

Through Victor Cousin, Hegel's philosophy became known in France. This young professor, who taught history of philosophy at the Sorbonne and the Ecole normale (teacher's college) in Paris, came to Germany in July 1817 with the aim of getting to know German philosophy. In Heidelberg he met one of Hegel's first adherents, F. W. Carové from Coblence, who spoke French and promised to initiate Cousin into Hegel's arcane work, which had just come out. The two of them could be seen in the castle gardens and on *Philosophenweg* (Philosopher's Road), holding the *Encyclopedia,* whose words and meaning Carové attempted to translate. Towards evening, they would drop in on Hegel "to consult the oracle," since Carové, as Cousin soon realized, understood nearly as little as Cousin himself.[71] With more and more problems and unanswered questions harassing him, Cousin took off for Munich to meet the remaining two of the "three most eminent philosophers of the present," Jacobi and Schelling.

A delightful reminiscence of Hegel's time in Heidelberg can be found in the notebooks of Baron Boris d'Uxkull. The Estonian landowner had been a cavalry officer in the Russian campaign against Napoleon. Now, battle-weary, he yearned for a profound revivification of his mind through scholarly learning. Attracted by Hegel's fame, he set out to master the essence of human knowledge from him within a short time, and came to Heidelberg in the spring of 1817:

"Having barely arrived and looked around a bit, I immediately paid a visit to the man about whose personality my imagination had created the wildest notions. With phrases carefully worked out beforehand (conscious as I was of my total lack of learning), I went, not without shyness but outwardly self-confident, to the Professor's home and, to my great amazement, found a very simple and unpretentious man, who spoke rather clumsily and brought forth nothing of any significance. Unsatisfied with this impression, although secretly attracted by Hegel's friendly reception and a certain characteristic of kind and yet ironic courtesy, I went—after registering for the Professor's courses—to the first bookshop I chanced upon, bought all of Hegel's works, and installed myself comfortably

Erfurt 19/9 22

[handwritten letter in German cursive]

A letter of Hegel's to Hinrichs.

in a sofa corner that evening in order to read them. Yet the further
I proceeded and the more attentive I tried to be, the less I understood what I was reading, so that after a few hours of struggling
with a single sentence and not managing to understand it, I felt
out of sorts and put the book away, but attended the lectures out of
curiosity. Yet I had to tell myself in all honesty that I couldn't
understand my own notes and that I lacked all preliminary instruction in these subjects. Now, in my tribulation, I went to Hegel,
who, after patiently hearing me out, amiably showed me the right
way, advising me to take various private lessons: Latin reading,
the rudiments of algebra, natural science, and geography. I did
this for six months, difficult as it was for a 26-year-old. Then I
reported to Hegel yet a third time; he received me with great kindness and couldn't help smiling when I told him about my propae-
deutical zigzagging. His advice was more definite now, his interest
keener, and I got something out of his courses. A colloquium held
by Doctor Hinrichs, in which disputants from all four faculties
participated and whose main theme was an exegesis of the *Phenomenology of Mind,* provided me with support. During the next two
semesters, Hegel visited me once or twice; I was at his place more
often and accompanied him on solitary strolls. He frequently told
me that our over-sophisticated era could be satisfied only by method, because it tames thoughts and leads to facts. Religion, he said,
is intuited philosophy, which in turn is nothing other than cog-
nizant religion; both used different methods to seek the same thing:
God. He told me never to trust any philosophy that is either
immoral or irreligious. He complained about not being understood
and repeated that logical knowledge had been brought to a close
and that everyone now had to make a clean sweep of things in
his own discipline since an overabundance of material existed side
by side with a lack of logical relationship and elaboration; that
only the arrogance of immaturity, the stubbornness of one-sided
understanding, the conceited and maudlin nature of sanctimonious
pseudo-salvation as well as the narrow-minded selfishness of privi-
leged obscurantism could possibly stop the dawning day."[72]

The abovementioned Doctor Hinrichs, whose philosophical col-
loquium Uxkull attended at Hegel's suggestion, was Hermann
Friedrich Wilhelm Hinrichs from Oldenburg, who became Hegel's
enthusiastic disciple. After acquiring his university lecturer's degree
(Habilitation) at Heidelberg in 1810, he became a professor in
Breslau and Halle and can be considered the first person to teach
Hegel's theories on an academic level, thereby founding the Hegelian
school. Another great admirer of Hegel was the theologian, Karl
Daub, the University's Vice-President, who had offered Hegel the

professorship at Heidelberg. In the summer term of 1821, Daub lectured to a huge audience on the *Phenomenology of Mind,* in which he saw a true substantiation of scholarship as well as theology.

At Creuzer's bidding, Hegel began to edit the philosophical-literary-philological section of the "Heidelberg Yearbooks for Literature"; his first contribution was a review of the recently published third volume of Jacobi's works. Immediately thereafter the Yearbooks published Hegel's *Critique of the Published Debates Held in the Assembly of the Diet of the Kingdom of Württemberg in 1815 and 1816* which Bülow describes as one of the best political pamphlets ever to appear in Germany. Here, after a lengthy pause, Hegel was once more in his element: the philosophy of constitutional law or politics.

In 1798, Hegel had attacked royal absolutism, but now he sided with the king, who wanted to give his people a modern constitution, which the diet, however, rejected. Hegel accused the representatives of letting themselves be richly paid for blatantly doing nothing and for achieving the exact opposite of what the French revolution intended to accomplish, that is, the creation of a state on the basis of reason. The diet could think only in historical terms, whether the latter were rational or not.

It was at this point that Hegel and his friend Paulus parted company forever; in fact, the warm relationship between the two families deteriorated into an open enmity full of hatred such as had existed between Paulus and Schelling as far back as Würzburg. Paulus wrote *for* the cause of the old diet; Hegel wrote against it. In regard to the controversy over the Württemberg constitution, the two men were absolute adversaries in the public eye. Paulus penned a "Philosophical Critique" of the matter, which Hegel, in a letter to Niethammer, labeled "extremely philistine and as common as common sense."[73] Through his personal activities, Paulus had gotten so involved in the constitution squabbles of his native province that in 1819, when he came to visit his ailing son in Stuttgart, King Wilhelm I had him arrested and ousted from the territory.

However, the chief event of the Heidelberg years was the publication of the *Encyclopedia of the Philosophical Sciences in Outline* in 1817. It constituted, although in summary form, a complete system of Hegel's entire philosophy. In 1827 and again in 1830, Hegel republished the work, each time revising and expanding it considerably. Anyone comparing the three editions with one another will have to agree with Rosenkranz, who feels "the creative breath of initial production" in the first version; yet the loss due to rewriting is made up for by the addition of legal philosophy and the development of the section on *Government and Religion.* Hermann Glockner, in his preface to the new edition of the Heidelberg Encyclopedia, justifiably says: "The 'political' man always remained fresh and alive in him: his legal philosophy as a comprehensive presentation of his theories of the objective 'Spirit' is certainly a further zenith of his work." [74]

As beautiful as Heidelberg was, Hegel did not want to settle there permanently. Naturally, his ego was strengthened by his return to academics and the growing appreciation of his philosophy; but he was waiting for the opportunity of developing his mature activity on a broader front. Charming as Baden was, it did not seem to offer him the necessary response to his theories. [75] And he was quite pleased by the thought that Berlin was still interested in him. The sand of Berlin, he would sometimes say, was more receptive ground for philosophy than Heidelberg's romantic surroundings. When Berlin finally made him an offer in a highly honorable fashion, Hegel wrote to his sister:

"I admit that the countryside I am leaving is beautiful, but one cannot sacrifice other circumstances essential to one's destiny for scenery. Berlin is a great focal point in itself, and philosophy has always been more of a necessity and more at home in the north of Germany than in the south." [76]

Perhaps Hegel had some other activity in mind besides academic teaching. In his youth, Hegel had already wondered "what hope there is, outside of dealing with theoretical works, to reach into the life of man." His talent for political philosophy is well known; but a remark in his letter of resignation to the Archducal Ministry of the Interior of Baden reveals that other thoughts were involved. His decision to transfer to Berlin was due to "primarily the prospect of various opportunities to change at an advanced age from the precarious function of teaching philosophy at a university and to be of use in a different field of endeavor." [77]

7

Berlin: The Culmination

Minister zum Altenstein Offers Hegel a Professorship
In Berlin, Hegel had not been forgotten. On November 3, 1817,
Friedrich Wilhelm III had created a special "Ministry for Religion, Education, and Medicine," headed by Baron von Altenstein,
who while serving under Minister von Stein had written a memo-
randum on educational reform. Altenstein thus became Minister of
Religion and Education, the first to bear this title *(Kultusminister)*
in Prussia. Boisserée calls him a "philosophizing minister" and an
"idealist such as I have never encountered among upper-class busi-
nessmen." Schleiermacher says of him: "Altenstein is evidently more
zealous about the education department than the religious section;
yet everything seems to be doing better than under Schuckmann."[78]

Altenstein knew Hegel not only through his writings but through
mutual friends as well. The interest he showed, a few weeks after
taking office, in the plan of getting Hegel to Berlin was indicated
by the great care devoted to the formulation of the written offer
sent to Hegel. After three drafts, all of which Altenstein threw away,
he penned a personal letter on December 26, 1817:

"Sir, you will be kind enough to recall how much I regretted
this past year that through a stroke of ill fortune you failed to come
to Berlin, since by the time our offer reached you, you had accepted
your present position in Heidelberg. However, your comments to
me and to our mutual friends permitted me to hope even then that
it would still be possible after a certain length of time to win you

over to Berlin. With the sincere wish that things are going well for you in your present situation, I do hope that your earlier attitude has not changed.

In taking over the supreme direction of public education, I consider one of the most important matters the finding of a worthy choice for the position left vacant by the death of Professor Fichte. Consequently, I herewith ask you to accept the teaching position at our Royal University as a Full Professor on the Philosophical Faculty. This position would involve a yearly salary of 2,000 Prussian thalers, and I would be glad to approve adequate reimbursement of your traveling expenses. I am not unaware of the obligations which might detain you in Heidelberg; however, your obligations toward scholarship are greater, and a wider and more significant range of activity is available to you here. You know what Berlin can offer you in this regard. And I hope that your expectations will be surpassed as soon as various projects are developed on which it is my duty to work. I would be much indebted for a speedy decision, and may I hope that this decision will fulfill a universal and decidedly sincere wish to have you here." [79]

Hegel's reply (January 24, 1818) shows him to be an experienced negotiator in dealing with ministers: his concern as a responsible head of family outweighed all other considerations. But who could blame the 47-year-old professor for wanting to be free at last of the burdens of petty economic worries? He had once told Creuzer that he had spent thirty years of his life in a troubled state of "fear and hope."

"Your Excellency's gracious letter, dated the 26th of last month and received by me on the 6th of this month, could not but arouse my keenest feelings for the benevolent sentiments Your Excellency has so kindly retained towards myself. The importance of the standpoint that Your Excellency has defined as well as the alteration of my present situation, in which I finally feel at home, demand most earnest deliberation. The good fortune of having Your Excellency at the head of educational affairs in the Royal Prussian States as well as Your Excellency's confidence in me have particularly supported me and helped me make up my mind to express my willingness to accept Your Excellency's gracious offer of a professorship of philosophy at the University of Berlin with the promised annual salary of 2,000 Prussian thalers. With Your Excellency's added promise of an adequate reimbursement of my traveling expenses there is little else to be desired on my part; however, my responsibility as a paterfamilias forces me to be frank with Your Excellency about this responsibility and to ask for kind consideration of it.

The general information about the significantly higher food prices in Berlin and especially about the exorbitant rents make me view as essential the inclusion in my salary of a certain quantity of produce as is the case with my present salary, which is thereby considerably greater than its nominal value, and would be even greater if living quarters were to be included as well. Since I have no knowledge of the extent to which the situation in Berlin can permit such an arrangement, I must leave the matter entirely to Your Excellency's discretion and will limit my wishes to such demands as are made possible by similar situations of other professors.

A more urgent consideration is the fate of my wife and my children in case of my death. The prospect of alleviation from the Widows' and Orphans' Fund here as well as the rather large admission fee and premiums I have paid will be lost when I leave my present position. In view of my lack of means, I must have some reassurance on this matter, and I therefore take the liberty of obediently asking Your Excellency to secure at least a proportionally suitable appropriation.

Although I thought I could leave the appropriation of the promised compensation for my traveling expenses to Your Excellency's gracious discretion, permit me to bring to Your Excellency's attention that I have recently had to furnish a new home at great cost and that within a short time another expenditure of this nature would be imminent. This circumstance imposes upon me the necessity of reassurance that I will not be faced with sacrifices beyond the range of my power; I must therefore name a sum, and if I go by the amounts granted by the [Heidelberg] government and considering the greater distance involved in moving to Berlin, I have to petition Your Excellency for the gracious settlement of 200 Friedrichs d'or. . . ."[80]

The minister's decisions proved quite generous. Hegel was to receive 2,000 thalers salary and 1,000 thalers indemnification for traveling, moving, and furnishing expenses:

"In regard to your other wishes, you may rest assured that there is a solid and well-organized Widows' Pension Fund for University Professors here; it is supported by a large subsidy from the State, and you are free to join. However, it will not be possible to provide you with free lodgings, partly because this emolument is given only to professors with whose further official functions it is connected, and partly because accommodations are lacking. However, the ministry believes that since your subsistence here will be well-founded and since attendance at your lectures will certainly not be lacking, you need not have any worries on this score. If, however, any problem should arise in the future, the ministry sets so

Karl Baron zum Altenstein.

great a store on gaining so profound a thinker with such a thorough scholarly background and such earnest and correct aspirations, that it will gladly contribute everything necessary to brighten up your residence here.

For the moment, it wishes nothing more than the complete satisfaction of the desires of so many who have been waiting so long for the Chair of Philosophy to be occupied. . . ."[81]

The Minister's goodwill remained manifest. Hegel constantly received extra financial support, either through respectable perquisites or else generous travel subsidies, and finally through the hiring of Carové and L. von Henning as his assistants.

Secure in his presentiments of imminent success, Hegel taught his fourth and last Heidelberg semester in the summer of 1818; his wife was taking the waters in Bad Schwalbach, and he wrote her joyful letters about the prospects of a happy future in Berlin.

The Minister's sister, Fräulein zum Altenstein, joined the search for a suitable home for Hegel. A house was found on the corner of *Leipziger Strasse* and *Friedrichstrasse*. Later, the Hegel family moved into the house where Hegel was to live until his death: "*Am Kupfergraben* number 4," on a branch of the Spree river, not far from the University and beyond the range of noise from the main thoroughfares. Rosenkranz enthusiastically drew a parallel, which Kuno

Fischer labeled "pointless": the house on *Kupfergraben* supposedly "had become as world-famous through [Hegel] as Sans souci through its royal philosopher."[82]

Hegel could be assured of a warm welcome at the University as well. His closest official colleague was the philosopher Karl Wilhelm Ferdinand Solger, translator of Sophocles, author of *Erwin*, and intimate friend of Ludwig Tieck's. The letter of welcome he sent to Heidelberg is permeated with a spirit of cheerful willingness for co-operation:

"When you are here, I hope I may succeed in winning your friendship! I won't make any long prefatory remarks about the sincere and profound esteem that your writings have always instilled in me. I have attempted to do the same work in my own fashion and using a different approach, and I hope that your reaction will not be too unfavorable. Perhaps we might even work together not only in harmony but on a joint project; I would appreciate such good fortune even more because it is not an everyday occurrence."[83]

Solger told Ludwig Tieck about his expectations in regard to Hegel's coming to Berlin:

"My courses are underway again: but attendance is small. I'm anxious to see what effect Hegel's presence will have. I'm sure many people believe that I find his appointment here disagreeable; yet I was the first to suggest his name and I can assure you that if I expect anything of him it is simply a greater stimulation of interest in philosophy, that is, something beneficial. When Fichte was here, I had ten times as many students as I do now. I esteem Hegel greatly and am remarkably in agreement with him on many points. In dialectics, both of us have independently followed almost the same route, or at least taken the same approach—and a new one at that. But I cannot tell whether we'll be in agreement on a few things peculiar to me. I would like once more to merge thinking into life, to articulate and show as being present the things that no amount of constructing and demonstrating can create, but merely purify and develop. . . ."[84]

Inaugural Lecture

In his inaugural speech on October 22, 1818, Hegel more or less echoed the words he had spoken on a similar occasion in Heidelberg; however, he modified them in terms of Prussia's political importance:

Earlier, he had viewed Prussia as an obstacle to the reconstruction of the old German Empire, but harsh as his opinion of the Prussian State may have been after the Battles of Jena and Auer-

Hegel lecturing (lithograph by F. Kugler).

stedt, he now unreservedly admired the way the Prussian government had prevented the extinction of the State in the worst of times, mobilizing political power for the good of all Prussia and working towards the state form; he admired the way Prussia had awakened to historical self-awareness as well as cognizance of her cultural mission and her task of teaching the people national consciousness.[85]

After greeting his audience, Hegel went on to say:

"At this point of time, those circumstances seem to obtain which augur the return of attention to and love of philosophy, so that this discipline, which almost completely lost its voice, may begin to speak again. For, a short time ago, it was in part the then current exigencies which gave the minor interests of everyday life such a great power over us, and it was in part the lofty interests of reality, the interests in the struggle to reconsolidate and preserve the political unity of national life and the State, a struggle which so absorbed all the energy of the intellect and the strength of all ranks of society as well as all outer resources, that the inner life of the mind could not find any respite; the World-Spirit [*Weltgeist*], so occupied with reality, so engrossed by external things, was prevented from turning inward and concentrating on itself, and from indulging and enjoying itself in its home territory. Well, after this torrent of reality had stopped and the German nation had rescued its nationality, the foundation of all living life, the time began in which, within the State, next to the governing of the real world, the free realm of thought blossomed independently. . . . And particularly this State which welcomed me, elevated itself by means of intellectual advantage to its authority in the real world and in politics, reaching the same level of power and independence as those states whose external resources were superior. Here, education in, and the flourishing of, science and scholarship are cardinal forces even in politics; and in this University, the university of the focal point [*Berlin*], the focal point of all intellectual training and of all scholarship and in this University, the university of the focal point [Berlin], vated pre-eminently.

However, intellectual life is not the only fundamental force in the existence of this state; now, more particularly, we are witnessing the sublime beginning of the great struggle of the people and its rulers for independence, for the overthrow of unfeeling foreign tyrants, and for freedom of mind, heart, and soul: the ethical power of the intellect felt its own energy, raised its banner, and asserted this feeling as the might and power of reality. We must regard as inestimable the fact that our generation has lived, acted, and produced in the grip of this feeling, in which all law, morals, and religion are concentrated. In such deep and universal endeavor, the intellect inwardly raises itself to its dignity, while the shallowness of life and the insipidity of interests perish, and the superficiality of judgment and opinion is exposed and vanishes. This profounder earnestness, which has entered the mind, heart, and soul, is the real basis of philosophy. Obstructions to philosophy are: on the one hand, the involvement of the mind in the problems of necessity and everyday life; and on the other hand, the vanity of opinions; the mind, captivated by this vanity, leaves itself no room for reason, which does not seek anything of its own. This vanity must banish itself to its own nothingness as soon as striving for substantial value becomes a necessity for mankind and such value alone asserts itself. . . .

Regarding German excellence in the cultivation of philosophy, [we may say this:] the state of the study of philosophy and the significance of its name in other nations show that the name has been preserved among them, but that the meaning has changed, and that the thing itself has degenerated and vanished, and to such an extent that hardly any memory or consciousness of it has remained. This discipline has fled to the Germans and survives only in them; we have been entrusted with the keeping of this sacred light, and it is our vocation to foster and nourish it and to make sure that the highest profession of man, the self-awareness of his essence, shall not die out and disappear. Yet even in Germany, the shallowness of the period preceding this renascence has gone so far as to imagine and assert that it has discovered and proved that there is no such thing as cognition of truth, and that God, the essence of the world and the mind, cannot be comprehended or understood; the mind (they claim) must stop at religion, and religion at faith, emotion, and premonition, devoid of rational knowledge; cognition (they claim) does not concern the nature of the absolute—of God and of that which is true and absolute in nature and mind, but rather only partially the negative; they claim that no truth is ever cognized, but rather that only untruth, the temporal and ephemeral, enjoys the privilege, as it were, of being cognized. . . . Thus, the thing that has always been considered the unworthiest and most ignominious, that is, the renunciation of the cognition of truth, has been elevated by our era to the highest triumph of the mind. When reason heard of this, its desperation was still linked with pain and melancholy; but soon, religious and ethical frivolity, and then the triviality and shallowness of the knowledge that dubbed itself enlightenment, freely admitted their impotence and asserted their arrogance in the total oblivion of higher interests; and finally, so-called critical philosophy supplied this ignorance of the eternal and the divine with a good conscience by asserting that it had proved that nothing [can] be known of the eternal and divine or of the true; this would-be knowledge even dared to call itself philosophy, and nothing was more welcome as giving character to the shallowness of knowledge, nothing was more willingly seized upon by it than this doctrine, by means of which this very ignorance, this shallowness and insipidity was passed off as excellence, as the goal and the product of all intellectual striving. Now they do not seek to know the truth but only phenomena, the temporal and accidental—only vain things, and it is this vanity which is spreading through and monopolizing philosophy. We can say that ever since philosophy began to grow prominent in Germany, things have never looked so bad for this discipline, that such an opinion, such renunciation of rational cognition has assumed such insolent proportions and achieved such diffusion—an opinion that has dragged its way in from the preceding age and stands in such opposition to genuine feelings, the new substantial Spirit. I welcome this dawning of a more solid Spirit; I invoke it; it is the only thing I deal with when I assert that philosophy must have substance and when I develop this substance for you; altogether I appeal to the mind of youth, for youth is the beautiful time of life, a time not yet enslaved in the system of the limited ends of necessity and still capable of the freedom of disinterested scholarly pursuit; nor is youth enslaved by the negative spirit of vanity, by the

Hegel's handwriting.

Arthur Schopenhauer
(painting by Ludwig
Sigismund Rühl).

unsubstantialness of purely critical exertion. A heart that is still healthy still has the courage to demand truth, and it is the realm of truth in which philosophy is at home, which it has built, and which we partake of by studying philosophy. Anything in life that is true and great and divine owes these qualities to the Idea; the goal of philosophy is to grasp the Idea in its true form and universality. . . .

Let me wish and hope that on the road we are taking I shall succeed in gaining and meriting your confidence; but for the moment I can ask only this, that you have confidence in scholarship, faith in reason, and faith and confidence in yourself. The courage of truth, faith in the power of the mind, is the primary requirement for the study of philosophy; man should honor himself and consider himself worthy of the highest. He cannot think highly enough of the stature and power of the mind; the closed and concealed essence of the universe has no power that can resist the courage of cognition; it [the essence of the universe] must disclose itself to him, revealing its riches and its depths and giving them up to him for his enjoyment."[86]

As of the winter semester of 1818–1819, Hegel taught an average of ten hours a week to an audience of 40 to 60. Besides his usual repertoire, he gave his first courses on the philosophy of religion and the philosophy of world history. In the winter of 1821, he started lecturing on *Natural Law and Political Science or Philosophy of Law as Based on my Textbook: Outline of the Philosophy of Law,* five times weekly from 5 to 6. For both lectures there were weekly study groups conducted by L. von Henning. The number of Hegel's students grew, with new ones constantly coming to the fore who were allowed to spread and cultivate the new doctrine under the eyes of the master. Thus, Hegel's teachings were regarded and received as a school philosophy.

Attendance at his lectures was considered a special recommendation not only for future teachers and professors, but for Prussian officials as well, particularly jurists. Thus, the Cultural Ministry's official in charge of education, Dr. Johannes Schulze (who had edited Winckelmann's works) came to Hegel's lectures regularly, not merely to cater to the Minister's wishes but out of his feelings of friendship for Hegel. He later recalled that Professor Hegel "never spared himself the trouble of helping me absorb the contents of all his lectures by showing me meticulous notebooks, which I copied. After class, he would give me the pleasure of his company in my home, or else we would take a walk and he would go more thoroughly into a discussion of any questions I might have about things in his lectures."[87] Hegel was telling the truth when, after his first year of teaching in Berlin, he wrote to Creuzer: "Here one's audience includes even majors, colonels, and Privy Councilors."[88]

In 1820, young Arthur Schopenhauer got his post-doctoral *Habilitation* in Berlin. A rather conceited teacher ("Posterity will set up a monument to me!"), he asked for permission to give his course at the same time as Hegel's main lecture so that he might see to whom the students would come: himself or Hegel. The experiment turned out disappointingly for Schopenhauer. Irritated, and weary of this test of strength, he retired: "Why should I spend another winter in Berlin? What have I got here? Not even enough students to make it worth the effort. My hovel is expensive and uncomfortable, and I don't care for it at all!"[89]

At first, Solger had written to Tieck that no one was talking about Hegel, who remained quiet and diligent. Evidently they had expected a different Hegel, for Solger said that "probably one of the stupidest parrots has come here, raising a terrible racket and telling the students to attend his classes for the good and salvation of their souls." But impressions speedily changed. Hegel became famous; the leading men of his time would not visit Berlin without going to his lectures or dropping in at his home on *Kupfergraben*.

Polemics Against Schleiermacher

Hegel's association with Schleiermacher, however, was less successful. Only a few weeks after Hegel's arrival, Schleiermacher had written: ". . . we will have to see how he does in the long run; there have already been a few complaints about his being incomprehensible, but this may pass. I'm happy that I can at least pull in my philosophical sails."[90] It had been part of Schleiermacher's duty as University President to inform the Ministry of the Senate's desire that Hegel be offered a professorship. Schleiermacher would gladly have prevented this, because a strong philosopher would be a hindrance to his philosophical and theological power. Thus, he was all the more intent on impeding any influence of Hegel's on the Berlin *Akademie der Wissenschaften (Academy of Sciences)*. The reason Schleiermacher gave for Hegel's not being made a member was: they didn't want a philosopher who might start a school, because this would only cause dissension; and after all, Fichte had not been included. But the pretext was much too flimsy. Hegel gave him tit for tat in a rather petty way. During an editorial meeting of the *Berlin Yearbooks for Scholarly Criticism (Jahrbücher für Wissenschaftliche Kritik)*, someone suggested asking Schleiermacher to join the staff. Hegel angrily jumped up, paced furiously to and fro, and mumbled to himself that this would be tantamount to ousting him. "After all the pro's and con's had been argued and shouted, the swelling din was finally stopped when someone pointed out that it would be more advisable not to ask Schleiermacher since he would be unable to accept, and this would be a slur on the Society's dignity."[91] As a result of the argument, Hegel alone determined the policy of the *Yearbooks,* and people spoke jestingly of the "Hegel Gazette."

Despite the tension between them, the two men managed to contain their antipathy in public; on one occasion, "at the Tivoli, chatting amicably arm in arm, they even took a toboggan ride together."

The triumph of intellect over crude forms can be demonstrated in two of Schleiermacher's and Hegel's letters. The following events had preceded them: After the murder of the writer, Kotzebue, De Wette had written a letter of consolation to the mother of the culprit, Sand, a student of theology, saying the deed had been committed by a pure, pious youth, who had acted to the best of his belief. De Wette was severely criticized and had to relinquish his professorship. At an evening conference of the "Lawless Society," to which both Hegel and Schleiermacher belonged, Hegel had defended the right of the government to dismiss a teacher (in this case, De Wette) as long as it continued paying him his salary. Schleiermacher expressed shock at this statement, and Hegel's rejoinder was equally irate. A few days later, Schleiermacher wrote to Hegel, skillfully complying with his request for the address of a certain wine dealer:

"So as not to forget one thing because of another. Dear Colleague: the agent of the Hesse House of Bordeaux is Rebstock, and he lives at Number 4, *Alexanderplatz.*

Incidentally, I am extremely obliged to you for immediately replying to the rude comment which should not have escaped me the other day; by doing so, you at least dulled the thorn left in me by my vehemence, which took me by surprise. I should like at some convenient opportunity to continue our discussion from the point at which it stood before those unseemly words were spoken. For I have too great an esteem for you not to wish that we may arrive at some agreement on a subject of such major importance in our present situation."

Hegel's answer was no less elegant:

"Thank you, Dear Colleague, first of all for the wine dealer's address in your note, which I received yesterday, and then for your remarks, which, while clearing up the recent unpleasantness between us, simultaneously settles the rejoinder produced by my excitement and leaves me with a decided increase of esteem for you. It is, as you observed, the current importance of this matter, which led me to begin a discussion in a society [meeting], a discussion which I am extremely interested in continuing with you so as to arrive at some reconciliation of our views."[92]

A further cause of controversy was offered by Hegel's polemics against Schleiermacher's "theology of feeling." In 1822, Hegel had written a commendatory preface to Hinrichs' book *On Religion in an Inner Relationship to Scholarship*. Rosenkranz made a disarmingly simple statement about the foreword, which he says was written under the sway of intense emotion, so that "stylistically, it contains in part a great beauty of racy anger." Feelings, writes Hegel, should never be raised to a principle, even for religion. Scholarship can even less afford to be based on feelings, and this holds true for theology insofar as it claims to be a science.

Then come the sentences that created a storm:

"Even [the thought] that this natural feeling is a feeling of the divine does not reside in the feeling as something natural. The divine is only in and for the Spirit, and the Spirit is, as was said above, not a natural life but the state of having been reborn. If feelings are to constitute the basic condition of the essence of man, then he would be on the same level as animals, for it is inherent in animals to have their condition in, and to live according to, feelings. If religion in a human being is founded only on a feeling, the latter has no other function than to be the *feeling of his dependency*, and thus a dog would be the best Christian, for it possesses this feeling most intensely and lives mainly in it. A dog even has feelings of 'salvation,' when its hunger is satisfied by a bone. The Spirit, however, finds liberation in religion and the feeling of its divine freedom; only a free mind has, or can have, religion; the thing that becomes confined in religion is the natural feeling of the heart, the specific subjectivity; the thing that becomes free in and precisely because of religion is the Spirit. In the worst religions, those in which bondage and thereby superstition are most powerful, it is the elevation to God that makes man feel, contemplate, enjoy his freedom, his infinity, his universality, that is, the Higher, which derives not from the feeling as such but from the Spirit. . . .

Religion frees man from the burden of himself; but it also frees him from the delusion of considering God a being alien to man. Letting oneself be determined by God is the same as letting oneself be determined by one's own being, which is essential and not accidental. The theologians love to talk about the *warmth* of the heart. But religion is not merely a warming of individuality, which in its particularity still keeps itself outside of God; it is the absolute fire in which the heart (insofar as it is, according to Christ's own expression, the principle of natural feeling) burns and the Spirit will arise from the destruction of everything perishable in it and unite with God as the Holy Spirit. We are used to seeing theologians contradicting themselves even more than philosophers do. They often preach so beautifully about the Covenant, the reconciliation with

God, the union of men with God and thereby with one another. But whenever we become serious about the union of the divine and the human, and whenever Christian truth is about to become reality, they quickly declare this striving to be a pantheistic aberration, view it as a subversion of government and church, and transmogrify pious awe of the divine into a terrorism of fear."[93]

Hegel kept up his polemic remarks on Schleiermacher's theology in lectures as well. And his rival voiced a bitter complaint in a letter to de Wette: "Hegel, just as he did in his preface to Hinrichs' *Philosophy of Religion* and in lectures, continues to inveigh against my animal ignorance of God and then to recommend Marheineke's theology exclusively. I take no notice; but it's certainly not pleasant."[94]

Friedrich Carl von Savigny, Professor of Roman Law, was being thrust more and more into opposition to Hegel. He gave vent to his anger in two letters to Creuzer:

"One of Hegel's chief followers, Henning, who is also your disciple, has just become a Doctor of Philosophy. You must read his dissertation *de systematis feudalis notione.* He shows that the Suevi and the Saxons are merely philosophical ideas, the former the idea of *generalitas,* the latter of *singularitas;* but because each and every thing must be a *totalitas* too, the Suevi were not entirely devoid of *singularitas* (devastation of neighboring countries) nor were the Saxons devoid of *generalitas* (their migrations). When all is said and done, I find Hegel's whole influence more and more questionable. Fichte did not possess or create any less dogmatism, but both he and his writings had a fresher, livelier spirit; I find Hegel far more narrow-minded, which also holds true for the strangely reconciliatory worldly wisdom he shows wherever people talk about the unpleasant events and institutions of recent and modern times. . . .

The philosophical enthusiasm of our students does seem to have calmed down a bit. What I take exception to in Hegel is by no means only his bumptious and superficial pronouncements on various disciplines outside his field . . . but also the fact that this self-same arrogance extends to everything in the world so that his zealous pupils disengage themselves from all religious association, and Fichte is thus greatly outstripped; furthermore [I object to] his totally warped, preposterous, chaotic behavior and speech in all non-scholarly matters, especially in the University's rather complicated relations with the government, on which subject his voice is merely one among those of the other professors."[95]

In June 1820, the Ministry made Hegel a regular member of the "Royal Board of Scholarly Examiners of the Province of Brandenburg." In this capacity, Hegel had to test all candidates for teaching in secondary school as well as applicants for the University, and—

an exceptionally time-consuming function—correct high school seniors' final examinations and papers written in requirement of the University teaching diploma. This office involved some degree of influence, but on the other hand, his advanced age made him feel the burden of such work, which took him back to the sphere he had been so happy to leave when transferring from Nuremberg to Heidelberg. He had different projects in mind, and so after two years, when he asked the Ministry to relieve him of this charge, his request was granted.

Hegel as Prussian Philosopher Laureate

In Berlin, Hegel worked first on the edition of his philosophy of law under the double title: *An Outline of Natural Law and Political Science* and *Basic Outline of the Philosophy of Law.* It appeared in 1821, under the imprint of the Verlag der Nicolaischen Buchhandlung. Despite the appended statement, *For use in connection with the lectures,* we should not forget that this was an attempt at presenting all practical philosophy in compact entirety. And the book really contains "Hegel's entire system in the positive element of practical reason."[96]

The preface acquired an unfortunate renown. In his hatred of the demagogical trend, Hegel included in his polemics the name of his former colleague in Jena and his predecessor in Heidelberg: Jacob Friedrich Fries, who had been suspended for taking part in the Student Meeting at Wartburg (in 1817) to protest against the reactionary policies of the German Confederation. Hegel called Fries the "commander-in-chief of all shallowness" and bitterly vituperated against his patriotic enthusiasm, his spirit of solidarity and friendship as "heart sop."

These remarks would have been better left unsaid. Even Rosenkranz, who usually manages to defend Hegel (claiming that "great men have the strength to articulate crucial things in a striking way that provokes anger") has to admit: "Woe to the man who gives offense. Others will enjoy his woe to the hilt." And Hegel had to pay for it. An implacable antipathy took root in all philosophical minds—whether they were followers of Kant, Jacobi, de Wette, or Schleiermacher.

Rudolf Haym, Hegel's second biographer, calls the foreword a "scientifically formulated justification of the Karlsbad police system and the persecution of demagogues." He goes on to say:

"In words of an exasperation and crudity reminiscent of Stein's contemporary onslaughts against men and ideas Stein did not know, [the preface] lashed out against anyone who dared to have independent views on the rationality of government and to translate these views into wishes and demands. Hegel takes as a representative of these theorizing and postulating politicians a man who should have been shielded from philosophical attacks not just because of his character but, far more so and absolutely, in light of his being declared an outlaw by the police. Yet the preface not only covered Fries' ideas with all the reproaches Hegel usually flung in divided attack on romanticism and enlightenment, on the Jacobi and Kantian schools; the preface not only labeled Fries the 'commander-in-chief' of prevalent 'shallowness,' a 'pettifogging advocate of arbitrariness,' and accordingly drew a caricature of his ideas; in this preface, philosophy actually joins forces with the police, progressing from attack and accusation to personal denunciation and the incitement of the public authorities. It is not Fries the philosopher but Fries the orator of Wartburg who is dealt with in the preface; Hegel explicitly approves of the fact that 'the governments have finally begun paying attention to this sort of philosophizing' and he hopes that neither officer nor title will become a talisman for principles 'giving rise to the destruction of both internal ethics and an honest conscience as well as public law and order.' And as proof of how rapidly the poison of police and official thinking was corroding contemporary minds, Hegel followed this first, ignoble step with a second, foolish step."[97]

This foolish action which Haym speaks of came about in the following way: In the February 1822 issue of the *Hallesche Allgemeine Literaturzeitung* (a literary periodical), a reviewer of *The Philosophy of Law* had criticized Hegel's unfair prefatory statements about Fries. "Why deliberately select the bad interpretation and cast suspicion on the words? Herr Fries, so far as we know, has not been fortunate, and the author's behavior toward him is tantamount to scorn and intentional abuse of a stricken man. Such conduct is not noble."

Hegel completely lost his temper. He copied down the closing lines of the review, and was so indignant as to demand ministerial protection against the "denunciation." He held it to be insufferable that a Prussian official should be inculpated in this fashion by a paper supported by the Prussian government and appearing in Prussia. Citing the review as an example of where too much freedom of press could lead, he demanded that the *Kultusministerium* award him damages.

Altenstein actually yielded to the point of advising the editors of the periodical to censor rigorously any reviews they published, and he even threatened to revoke their license in case they refused. However, the Minister wrote to Hegel that if he wanted damages he would have to go to a court of law.[98]

But back to the preface of *The Philosophy of Law* and a further offense that "alienated all hearts" from Hegel. Rosenkranz admits that "all who had Prussia's future in view turned suspiciously from Hegel, whose politics [they deemed] too restricted and too dependent on his relation to Prussia as he found it."[99] What was so offensive about Hegel's words?

Hegel worked from the premise that philosophy must grasp the present and not postulate an after-life. The State, a thing of the present, rules as a realm of freedom rather than of arbitrary power, and by means of laws. Wherever legality holds sway, rationality is involved, that is, recognizable and knowable reason. Nothing could be more erroneous or more foolish than to want to replace political understanding and science with so-called demagoguery. Now since law is the only thing in the world to have stability, permanence, and effectiveness, one may make the valid statement: "Anything rational is real, and anything real is rational."

Just as Bacon called truth "the daughter of time," Hegel felt that "philosophy grasps its current era in thought." Philosophy's vocation is not to make reality but to cognize prevalent and present-day reality. "Understanding that which is, is the task of philosophy." Philosophy presupposes reality at a point at which the development to a zenith is complete. Thus the foreword to the *Philosophy of Law* closes with the famous line: "When philosophy paints its gray on gray, then the form of life has grown old and can no longer be rejuvenated with gray on gray, but only cognized; it is only when twilight sets in that the owl of Minerva begins to fly."

However, it was not this statement that invited criticism, but the earlier one: "Anything rational is real, anything real is rational." It did not help matters that Hegel tried to qualify his words in the second edition (1827), explaining that by reality he did not mean merely the empirical realm—existence mixed with chance, that is, with bad things and things that ought not to be—but rather existence as identical with the notion of reason. For if common phenomena, immediate reality, are to be included in the real, then there can be no question that immediate reality can be highly irrational.

Hermann Glockner's apologia is equally unconvincing: "Neither the Prussian state existing at that time nor the transitory historical moment was meant, but rather that 'eternal present' which exists 'always' and contains preserved in itself the entire past." Still, Glockner does concede that the dubious line about the rationality of reality poses a difficulty "which has never been completely solved even by orthodox Hegelians."[100]

The most vehement critic was once more Rudolph Haym in his biography of 1857. He wrote that Hegel "in anti-demagogical and anti-subjectivistic zeal" had "come out with the classical statement of the spirit of restoration, the absolute formula of political conservatism, quietism, and optimism." Haym goes on to say: "It was quite in order, I think, that a government making the bad choice of reactionary politics and yet vain about scholarly protection eagerly seized a hand offered so unconditionally by philosophy. Hegel, as far as I can see, totally deserved Altenstein's 'certificate' declaring him, as it were, the philosopher laureate of restoration and the Prussian state. As far as I can see, in contrast to that famous statement [in Hegel's preface] about the rationality of all reality, everything that Hobbes, Filmer, Haller, or Stahl ever taught was relatively liberal and progressive. The divine-right theory and the idea of *oboedentia absoluta* are innocent and harmless compared with the terrible doctrine which hallows the status quo for being the status quo."[101]

It may admittedly be a malicious procedure to pluck that one sentence out of the foreword "in order to display it as a clear-cut statement to all readers before they tackle the work itself" (Gans); but to accuse anyone taking the dictum at face value of being narrow-minded is just as wrong. It was no coincidence that the Prussian government based its political conception on Hegel's philosophy, and not only on his philosophy of law, but on his philosophy of religion as well. State and philosophy, because of the common nature of knowledge, form a close alliance against religion. For the State, like philosophy, is that which religion is not: self-knowing rationality. Thus the description of Hegel as the "official Prussian political philosopher" was not slanderous. He considered himself a professor among professors, as witness the title he conferred upon himself in a letter to his wife (!): "And I, Professor Royal *publ. ordin.* at the Royal University of Berlin (professor of a special subject, philosophy, the most special of all special subjects). . . ."[102]

Robert Heiss is not sure that Hegel fully deserves Haym's rebuke ("Hegel's philosophy resolved itself into the philosophy of restoration.") Heiss claims that anyone measuring Hegel's philosophy of law by the famous and infamous tenet, *anything real is rational,* will fail to comprehend what new perspectives were opened by his philosophy of law. Thus, one must regrettably ascertain (says Heiss) that all critics, barring none, have made the mistake of "assuming without a second thought that Hegel wrote this work for external reasons and to defend the contemporary Prussian State." Yet it is odd that Heiss himself does not arrive at a new position. His interpretation of the preface culminates in the reproach that Hegel, in applying his principle of dialectics to the relationship between theory and reality, became ambivalent, because he thereby recanted his earlier opinions. "The Berlin Hegel disavows the statements made by the younger Hegel." Whereas in his youth Hegel had written to Schelling that theory is the battering ram to move reality, he now inveighed against the men who wanted to teach the State how it ought to be. Philosophy (he claimed) always arrived too late to teach how the world should be. "Hegel capitulates to reality; theory never marches at the head of reality; it always lags along behind."[103]

Lectures on the Philosophy of History

In the last decade of his life, Hegel published only individual essays as well as the written elaboration of two great new lecture-courses: *Philosophy of Religion* and *Philosophy of World History*. His works and lectures now formed a complete system. This system was primarily historico-philosophical. One can say that "Hegel's conception of history is metaphysical and his metaphysics historical." Moreover, we should bear in mind that the historical played a great part in Hegel's philosophy of religion and his aesthetics and that he gave his course on the History of Philosophy annually, developing and improving it from year to year.

It is important to ascertain the role of the historical, for it helped make Hegelianism comprehensible to a wider audience. The method of dialectics first became known by its application to history. Previously, most people could scarcely form an idea of the logical triad of thesis, antithesis, and synthesis. Now, much of what Hegel had taught became clear; his lecture rooms filled up. But some danger was involved: the controversies raging in favor of or against Hegel took place mainly on a level created by the more or less popular conception of his philosophy of history.[104]

The lectures on the philosophy of world history are based on the principle "that reason rules the world, that therefore world history advances rationally." The course of world history is a meaningful process with a definite purpose. Seeing significance and purpose in history means grasping it significantly. "Thus, the aim of world history is that the mind acquire the knowledge of what it itself really is and that it make this knowledge concrete, realize it for an existing world, and produce itself as something objective." The means employed by the *Weltgeist* to make its purposes come true are the actions of individual men. However, above the unhistorical individuals stand the world-historical personalities, whom the World Spirit uses as instruments. "The new world circumstances, the deeds they perform, appear as their own creations, interest, and work. But they have right on their side, for they are endowed with judgment: they know what the truth of their world and their time is, what the Notion [*Begriff*] is, the next issuing universal, and the others, as was said, rally around their standard, because they verbalize the truth about their time. They are the most impressive persons in the world and know best what matters; and whatever they do is right. The others, feeling this, must obey them. Their words are the best that can be spoken, their deeds the best that can be done."

Yet they only imagine that they are pursuing their individual purposes; in reality, the "cunning of reason is using them for universal purposes." They are merely "representatives of the World-Spirit." The fact that in their passions they may trample innocent flowers on the way and cause a great deal of destruction bothers (according to Hegel) only servants or pedants, who lack any understanding of true greatness. Individuals are abandoned and sacrificed. Their freedom consists only in annihilating their arbitrary isolation and being integrated in a universal ethical whole. It is not individual happiness that is important: "World history is not the basis for happiness. Periods of happiness are blank pages in it."

Critical comments on these lines are unnecessary. One can read the ironical observations made by Kirkegaard, who while conceding that some sort of destiny rules over history, stubbornly denied that Professor Hegel had any insight into the plans of providence. Hegel, however, regarded the philosophical writings of his predecessors from Descartes to Fichte as mere stepping-stones, developmental stages in the history of philosophy leading to some unknown point; he considered his own philosophy the consummate conclusion to this historical process, the unification and *Aufhebung* of all earlier knowledge and cognition. Advances would still be made, but as on a plateau there would be no more striving upwards. Hegel notwithstanding, this belief itself might be offered as a demonstration of the "cunning of reason," which turned his original aim into something far different from what his "subjective spirit" imagined.

Aesthetics and Philosophy of Religion

Between 1835 and 1838, Hotho published *Hegel's Lectures on Aesthetics.* Hegel's philosophy of art evinces an astonishingly excellent taste. Earlier, in 1805, he had told Voss that if he were ever permitted to teach in Heidelberg, he would lecture on aesthetics in terms of a *cours de littérature.* It was only thirteen years later that he kept his promise. And in Berlin he added richly to his Heidelberg lectures, using illustrative material provided by the capital city's art treasures, exhibitions, and theaters, and by vacation trips to galleries in Dresden, Vienna, Paris, and the Netherlands. Thus the *Aesthetics* became the most magnetic and most popular of Hegel's courses in Berlin. The serenity and clarity of art may have helped to tone down his more ponderous philosophy of the *Geist.* Hegel states categorically that the province of artistic beauty is different from that of thought, and that grasping its activity and its products demands a different organ than

Goethe (chalk drawing by Ferdinand Jagemann).

scholarly and scientific thinking does. Hegel saw as inherent in art its ability to translate itself into objective existence; when leaving its subjectivity, art—unlike religion—is not required to reach into other areas or employ any means other than its own. The inner being of religion can be obscured in cult and dogma; but the most intrinsic essence of art is revealed all the more purely and completely in the objectivity of the art work. This is why (according to Haym) Hegel misunderstood and disparaged the specific nature of religion while recognizing it in art.[105]

Hegel's religious philosophy culminated in the sentence: "The substance of the Christian religion, the highest developmental stage of any and all religion, coincides completely with the substance of true philosophy." All philosophy is nothing other than the proof of the focal truth of Christianity: that God is love, Spirit, substance, subject, and a process of eternal return to itself. Religious philosophy sees that its specific nature is to concentrate into what is at once a summit and summation the truth permeating general philosophy. It raises itself to insight—insight into the corresponding relationships of God-to-man and man-to-God. More precisely: "Man knows about God only insofar as God knows about himself within man; this knowledge is God's self-awareness as well as God's knowledge of man, and this knowledge that God has of man is man's knowledge of God; man's spirit in knowing God is merely God's spirit itself."

In this definition, the content of religious truths has thinned down to a shadow and been cheated of its own interest. The panlogical character of Hegel's philosophy triumphs, revealing itself to be, as Glockner himself grants, "a doctrinaire rationalism that totally fails to understand the essence of the irrational." [106]

The most important chapter, dealing with *Cult,* was added to the *Philosophy of Religion,* only to be entirely deleted in the end. "Religious conception finds recognition only insofar as it transmutes itself into philosophical dogma. Cult attains its full truth only when formed into ethics. Only the State is consummate worship. The State is to the Church as philosophy is to religion; State and Church are not 'opposed in the contents of truth and rationality, but are dissimilar in form.' " Philosophy is thus "a separate sanctuary, and those who serve it form an isolated priesthood, who may not associate with the world and who must guard the possession of truth. It is the task of the temporal empirical present to learn how to find its way out of its own schism and [this task] is of no immediate practical concern to, or business of, philosophy." [107]

Philosophy, for Hegel, is not just absolute knowledge for man, but the consummation of God's reality. Thus, at the end of Hegel's system, the philosophy of philosophy, the self-knowledge of human and divine spirit, is faced with the highest task ever accorded to it by a philosopher.

Hegel and Goethe

Of all those who were kindly disposed toward Hegel and interested in his work, we must mention Goethe. The friendly relationship went as far back as Hegel's years in Jena, but it was based on a harmony between essential features of their total concept of the world. In 1817, Boisserée had sent Goethe the *Encyclopedia* paragraphs in which Hegel had condemned Newton's and supported Goethe's theory of color. Goethe was very happy about it and wrote on July 8, 1817:

"Your highly welcome and positive way of declaring yourself in favor of the ancient theory of color, which only I have propounded anew, requires my sincere gratitude doubly and triply, since in my decision to once more publicly express my opinion on these matters I am looking about for friends and sympathizers." [108]

During Hegel's Berlin period, the exchange of ideas between the two men recommenced. Goethe had sent Hegel a copy of his treatise on *Entoptic Colors;* the philosopher thanked him in a long letter, praising Goethe's understanding of nature and his grasp of the essence of phenomena as the "primary phenomenon" *(Urphänomen).* To explain the following charming gesture, we must add that "entoptic" colors are defined as those that "are to be seen within certain solid bodies." Goethe sent Hegel a delicate tumbler tinted yellow and containing a piece of black silk which made the yellow seem blue—a kind of symbol of Goethe's theory of colors. The dedication read: "The primary phenomenon most courteously begs the absolute to receive it graciously."

In a letter to Reinhard, Goethe tells about "a desirable statement made by Professor Hegel in Berlin; for some time now, this man, with his marvelously keen and acute mind, has been a friend to my ideas on physics, especially the chromatic ones.

"His comments on my entoptic essay were so incisive that I really find the work more lucid than before. Since you, too, showed such faithful and consistent interest in it, you will probably be glad to read a digest of the most relevant passages. . . ."

Goethe wrote to C. F. L. Schultz on March 10, 1825:

"I should not hold back an enormous pleasure that I experienced in the past few days. Professor Hegel wrote me a letter that did me a great deal of good. He referred to my last scientific *cahier,* particularly the *Entoptic Colors.* The singularly intelligent man illuminated this chapter, like my whole *Chromagenesie,* in such a way that my work became really lucid to me for the first time. It came at a highly desirable moment, since I was beginning to sift, and do a bit of editing on, my papers that had been amassing for the past ten years—I am planning to use them for my next piece." [109]

On October 16, 1827, en route back from Paris, Hegel stopped off in Weimar to see Goethe. The writer introduced him to Riemer, Zelter, and Archduke Karl August, who happened to be there. Hegel wrote his wife an account of it:

"Yesterday evening, I arrived here during sunset. After getting settled, off I went to the destination of my side-trip, to see my old and honored friend. The house was aglow, the Archduke had announced that he was coming to tea; but I sent notice of my arrival all the same. Goethe welcomed me in the warmest and friendliest terms imaginable; I had a great deal to tell him. After half an hour, the old Archduke came. I must add one important fact, that besides Riemer, I met Zelter at Goethe's home. Goethe introduced me to the most gracious gentleman [the Archduke], and I sat down next to him on the sofa—I think I was even on his right side. He asked about Paris—he is somewhat deaf— . . . and thus we spent the evening (Zelter and Riemer were smart enough to sit in the adjacent room) as well as we could in conversation with the old gentleman until 9:30. Goethe remained standing all the while, and I gradually realized that the Archduke was slightly deaf, and that during a pause we were not supposed to speak but were to wait until he thought of something to say. Otherwise, everything went smoothly, I had to endure being riveted to my sofa for a couple of hours. The Archduke recommended my visiting his botanical garden in Belvedere. This morning at ten, Zelter and I drove out—Goethe had lent us his carriage. The garden is really large and sprawling. The Duke is quite a botanist—there are fine samples of plants to be seen there—of course, neither of us was well-versed enough to duly appreciate everything. At noon we were back here. I visited Herr and Frau von Schwendler, who swamped me with regret that you hadn't come along and that I was letting Goethe monopolize me, etc. Next, a stroll through the beautiful park, down the old familiar paths I had walked along twenty-five years ago, a salutation to the banks of the tiny Ilm river and its quiet waves, which have heard many an immortal song. At 2 p.m., luncheon at Goethe's home, a first-rate meal honored by excellent appetites. Goethe's daughter-in-law, expecting her baby at any moment, remained invisible, and was thus not at the table—her sister Fräulein von Pogwisch was quite cheerful. Privy Councilor Vogel, the doctor, a certain D. Eckermann (Goethe's secretary), the two grandchildren, the son, Zelter, and I—I sat next to Goethe, with Fräulein von Pogwisch at my right; the Weimar guests were quieter, but we were sociable, chatty, and ate and drank heartily. I had to tell Goethe about political and literary views and interests in France; everything was of great interest to him. He is quite hale and hearty, still the old Goethe, that is, ever youthful, somewhat calmer—such an honorable, good jovial head that one tends to forget the great man of genius and the inexhaustible energy of his talent. True friends that we are, I never observe how he acts or what he says; on the contrary, we are on excellent terms, and I don't associate with him for the glory and fame of seeing him or hearing him say something, etc. After lunch, Goethe's son expressly told me that Goethe had been pleased at the prospect of my stopping off on the way back from Paris. The son spoke a great deal about his own life and his feelings toward his father in every respect; considering Goethe's age and way of life, one has to congratulate him for enjoying such love and care, and we must respect and cherish his son for it. Tonight, I went to the theater, and now I'm writing to you, and most of all I must add a bit about our plans, or rather our decision to finally go home. Goethe would like Zelter and myself to stay at least until tomorrow; consequently, we're leaving the day after. Zelter is just as satisfied as I am that we are continuing the trip together. But since both of us are getting to be elderly gentlemen and find comfort pleasant and useful, we don't have the courage to take the express coach . . . instead, we will use the cabman whom we have already hired, get underway on Friday, and—God willing— arrive [in Berlin] on Sunday, where, returning from his colorful travels to the uniformity of domestic life, your Odysseus will take you in his arms."[110]

Goethe, in a letter to Knebel, expressed his regret that Hegel could not remain longer:

". . . whatever appears unclear and abstruse in the printed disclosures of such a man, since we cannot directly assimilate it to our needs, immediately becomes our property in a vivid conversation because we realize that we agree on basic ideas and views and would like to draw nearer to each other and unite in joint development and elucidation."[111]

Two years later, returning from Karlsbad to Berlin, Hegel visited Goethe for the last time. "I spent five or six days in old, cordial friendship with Schelling in Karlsbad, after a tour of Teplitz and Prague—then Weimar, to the 80-year-old youth, and Jena (where your old pranks broke the windows)."[112]

Hegel's Travels in Letters to His Wife

After each summer semester, Hegel, in need of rest, would seek relaxation and change on shorter or longer trips, for which the Ministry granted him very generous financial assistance. In the summer of 1822, the Minister wrote to him:

"I gratefully realized that last year, on the sole basis of my guaranteeing some financial support of the journey you were to take at my wish to restore your health, you actually started out; I was sorry that it took me so long to fulfill my promise. The delay was caused by my wish to procure some assistance for you toward the same purpose this year. I am very happy to inform you in the enclosed official note that I succeeded in procuring not only a grant of 300 thalers as remuneration for last year, but an equal sum for this year, that is to say, a total of 600 thalers. I hope that, in connection with my guarantee for the future, this sum will completely set your mind at ease and that you will be able to take at least a short pleasure trip this year. If possible, grant yourself such relaxation and refreshment after your strenuous and successful work."[113]

Hegel had no great desire to go off traveling, and if he had had his way he would have remained at home alone, dividing his vacation between his family and his studies. But the money was intended for holiday trips, he had accepted it, and so he had to go. More than once, concern for his family had nearly made him turn around and go back after the first day, and although travel impressions increased his spirit of adventure, he felt as if he were "actually always en route home."[114]

On September 15, 1822, he began his journey through Cologne, Brussels, Ghent, Antwerp, Amsterdam, Hamburg, and back to Berlin. One of his first pupils and most grateful friends from the Jena period lived in the Netherlands—Peter Gabriel van Ghert, who was in charge of education and schooling at the Dutch Ministry of Culture. Upon hearing of Hegel's difficulties in Jena, he had immediately written a letter in German that bristled with mistakes but was filled with affection for and gratitude toward his honored teacher: he wanted to get Hegel a chair of philosophy in Holland with a salary of 6,000 gulden; his offer included a connection with a well-paying publishing house, which was willing to put out Hegel's works. The letter assured Hegel that Ghert was imbued with the most venerable feelings of esteem and friendship and was more interested in everything concerning Hegel than the whole rest of the world.

Since Hegel's wife never accompanied him on his trips, his numerous letters to her contain excellent as well as peculiar travel descriptions, which reveal an unknown aspect to his character. From Cologne he wrote:

"Cologne is extremely vast—I immediately sought out the cathedral, the slender proportions, their stretching quality, not so much a climbing as a flying upwards—are a sight to see and admire as the conception of *one* man and the enterprise of a city; a different state of things, a different world of men, a different time vividly strikes the eye in every way. It is not the practical that constitutes the joy and pleasure, the satisfied need, but a vast strolling about in lofty, self-sufficient halls, which are, as it were, totally indifferent to men's using them for whatever purpose; an empty opera house, like an empty church, is incomplete—this is a towering forest, an intellectual and artistic one—standing complete unto itself, and whether or not men creep or walk about below doesn't matter to it in the least—it is unto itself what it is, it is meant to exist for itself, and any Rhine voyager going about in it or praying, with oil-cloth knapsack and—unlit—pipe, is lost within as is the church warden; the moment people enter here, they merely vanish." [115]

From Aix-la-Chapelle (Aachen), he reported:

"In Aachen, I went to see the cathedral first, and sat down on Charlemagne's throne; there are double slabs of marble on each side and on the back: smooth, one-and-a-half inches thick; they were coated with gold-sheet, in which stories had been engraved, and a few parts are still preserved. On this throne, 300 years after his death, Charlemagne was found (I think by Emperor Frederick) sitting up, dressed in his imperial vestments, with his crown on his head, his scepter in one hand and his imperial globe in the other; these objects were added to the crown jewels, and his remains were buried. I sat down, as anyone else might, on his throne, on which thirty-two emperors had been crowned, according to the churchwarden, and the whole satisfaction consists in having sat there."[116]

And from the Hague:

"The churches as you know—in Ghent, Antwerp, must be seen if one wants to see sublime, rich Catholic churches—huge, vast, Gothic, majestic—stained-glass windows (the most splendid I have ever seen are in Brussels); on the columns, life-sized marble statues placed at a certain height, or else reclining, sitting—by the dozens; paintings by Rubens, Van Eyck, and their disciples, large works, two or three dozen splendid works in one and the same church; marble columns, bas-reliefs, latticed pews and confessional boxes, a half or even whole dozen in the Cathedral of Antwerp, each pew or box adorned with four life-sized, excellent wood carvings (I thought of the Annunciation in Nuremberg); the town halls are just as peculiarly Gothic. In Antwerp, we were on our feet for four hours in the morning; I have been sweating for eight days, in Waterloo I thought to myself that I hadn't sweated quite as much as the French and the Allies had. In Antwerp, my dear friend Herr van Ghert and I parted company, he returned to Brussels with instructions to inquire whether any more letters from you had arrived, and to forward them to me in Amsterdam."[117]

Hegel was full of praise for Holland:

". . . What a lovely country! This is a country for strolling, green meadows everywhere with contented, well-fed cattle and no whip-holding cowherds behind them—long parks filled with oaks and beeches; country villas—Holland is the most densely populated land in the world, but there are few villages in the flatlands. Brabant, a fertile area full of villages. Haarlem, clear, large, and lovely as the others, lies on Haarlem Lake. For all the beautiful things and places I have seen and am seeing, there are just as many, equally beautiful ones, that I have not seen, but I have seen the most important, the finest and the best. Every city is rich, dainty, and clean. I still cannot tell where they keep the common folk and the poor, especially in the Hague; no dilapidated houses, palsied roofs, rotten doors, broken windows anywhere. In the Hague and generally here, all the streets are filled with the finest shops, in the evening all the streets are lit up by their illuminations, endless assortments—gold, silver, porcelain, tobacco, bread, shoes—everything perfectly arranged in booths."[118]

Two years later, Hegel—once more alone—traveled to Vienna via Prague during the autumn weeks of 1824. In Vienna, he found everything agreeable and interesting: the marvelous art treasures and collections, the public parks, and most of all the Italian Opera, which threw him into the greatest of raptures and whose beauty he could not laud highly enough:

"Good morning, my dear!—in Vienna—yes, Vienna; but unfortunately you are not in Vienna . . . (I arrived at the inn at 7 a.m.) at 7:30—off to the Italian Opera, for Madame Milder, whom I have to mention again below, had recommended it so highly. An opera by Mercadante, Madame Fodor was not in the cast—but what male voices! Two tenors, Rubini and Donzelli, what throats, what grace, charm, volubility, strength, sonority, they simply must be heard!— a duet of the greatest force. Lablache, a bass, did not sing a leading role, but all the same, how I admired his fine, powerful, and charming voice. Yes indeed, these male voices have to be heard for their sonorousness, purity, power, complete freedom, etc., etc. They also have a German singer, her name is Eckerlin, she's got fine, full strong mediants, which reminded me of Madame Milder, but only Madame Milder could be a match for, and hold her own against, those three male voices. Madame Fodor is singing in *Othello* today. As long as I have enough money left to pay for the Italian Opera and the trip home—I'm staying in Vienna! Off to the opera and a pas de deux by two Parisians—in every way as good as the Berliners—when Berlin ballerinas stick out just a right angle, it becomes obtuse. Then I went home, where, to our mutual warm pleasure, I found Lilli and Klein (Parthey's young wife, being indisposed, was in her room); I'm very glad of it, they are here for a week, and we've agreed to go about together; they were surprised that I was coming from the Italian Opera, for the past three days they've spent every evening at the Punch and Judy show and the German Theater and haven't even seen or heard the Italian Opera!!"[119]

With the approach of the summer holidays of 1827, Hegel began planning a trip to Paris and wrote to Cousin, who had been politically incriminated in 1824 and arrested in Dresden. Due to Hegel's speaking on his behalf to the Prussian Minister of the Interior, Von Schuckmann, Cousin was released but remained under political surveillance in Berlin for some time. Upon hearing of Hegel's travel plans, he responded to them with ardent and practical enthusiasm, putting himself, his home, and his time completely at Hegel's disposal.

Hegel's route led through Trèves, Luxemburg, and Verdun to Paris, where he stayed in the Hôtel des Princes; his room being too expensive, he moved into a *chambre garnie,* and every day he and Cousin would go sightseeing. Although he reported new impressions, his wife to her astonishment correctly noticed that his letters from Paris were not as bright or communicative as those from Vienna, three years earlier.

"Now, my dear, about this capital of the civilized world, in the study of my friend Cousin, who (let me speak of it first) gave me your dear letter of the 20th of this month, so that I finally received news of you and the children, whose letter also warmed my heart. . . .

. . . I am encircled by a library, in which I can go more deeply into and make the acquaintance of the interests and viewpoints of the [French] mind—of course I don't really have enough time; so far, the weather has been continuously beautiful, and rainy days are simply not to be wished for. . . .

. . . Paris is a city of ancient riches, in which for many centuries kings enamored of art and splendor, most recently Emperor Napoleon, and wealthy aristocrats, and then a busy and industrious people, have amassed all sorts of riches in every possible way: there are scores of palaces and public institutes—every faculty of the university, for example, has a palace something like our university building. The *Halle au vin* [wine market], a building consisting only of wine vaults, is a grandiose institute. . . . The whole city is naturally three, four, ten times larger, vaster, and more comfortable than Berlin, all of it to be used directly by the public, and yet everything protected in such a way as to ward off damage. I particularly wish you could visit the *Palais royal,* the Paris in Paris; the endless throng of boutiques and the endless wealth of merchandise, beautiful jewelers' shops, are astounding. Yet every street is garnished with every sort of superabundance and splendor; you can get anything anywhere . . . and any dealings with the people are simple, reasonable, and honest. But a person should not indulge in fault-finding. The churches, the Pantheon or Ste. Geneviève—a new church—and the old cathedral of Notre Dame are grandiose examples of architecture. . . .

The picture gallery is in the Louvre: a long, straight room with a vaulted ceiling—both walls are covered with paintings—a corridor extending almost beyond the reach of the eye, a quarter-of-an hour long; a few days earlier, Cousin and I had gone through it quickly. Yesterday I wanted to begin a closer study and viewing, but as it turned out, there was time only yesterday and today—starting tomorrow, the Museum is . . . closed due to preparations for the exhibit of present-day masters; there is a great wealth, and there are famous pictures one has seen a hundred times in etchings, paintings by the most illustrious masters, Raphael, Correggio, Leonardo da Vinci, Titian, et al.

The French are generally calmer and preciser in the articulation of their feelings than we [Germans] are, especially you; how often do I tell you to speak and treat of a thing without emotion; yet your liveliness often suits you well. Otherwise, I have seen, and spoken to, few people; at the moment, there is no one in Paris. Cousin wanted to take me to the home of the Duchess de Montebello, but then we didn't go; she is ailing. Everyone's out in the country; the silly German habit of making it a point of honor to have spoken to so-and-so and so-and-so is completely out of place here. . . .

This week, my Parisian life has not produced any great variety of things; on the contrary, it has been extremely uniform, and it is primarily about this uniformity that I must write, so that you may not indulge in useless worries and so that you may hear about my temporary indisposition directly from me. . . .

You observed that I don't write with the same ardor and enthusiasm from Paris as from Vienna, and that you have told our friends a great deal. This may be so; but everything I write is too fleeting to be very informative. Besides, you must take into account the fact that my indisposition made me lose a good deal of time, and then everything is so terribly far away that a man has to be physically quite fit to take in different things and [I] would have to remain a much longer time for the sake of more thorough contact and penetration. It is a highly interesting place; but a few weeks barely suffice just to overcome one's stupefaction and grow accustomed to all the splendor and variety here . . . in short, one would have to spend six months in Paris to feel at home with all the things interesting one more deeply, and, by way of acclimatization, to lose one's interest in the things that one at first finds remarkable and worth seeing. Cousin has often laughed at me for seeing and finding remarkable the things that a tourist's conscience and the *Manuel des Étrangers* imposed upon me to view. . . .

But now I have to stop, just as I have stopped sightseeing in Paris; I cannot exhaust writing about the remarkable sights, nor could I exhaust everything within four weeks like tourists who wish to discharge their duty and do a thorough clock-work job of sightseeing. . . ."[120]

The pleasant homeward journey with Cousin led through Brussels, where Hegel saw his friend Van Ghert again, Louvain, Liège, Aix-la-Chapelle ("I visited the cathedral by candlelight and sat on Charlemagne's throne once more") to Cologne, which was as far as Cousin accompanied his friend. A few years later, Cousin reported that Hegel, upon seeing merchants standing at the entrance to the cathedral and hawking holy medals and candles, angrily cried out: "There's your Catholic religion and the scandal it offers us! Will I die before I see all this perish?"

At this point it might be apropos to consider some of Hegel's religious attitudes. A letter of his from Elberfeld contains a remarkable utterance about what was for him a disagreeable controversy in Berlin, of which we should not refrain from giving an account. "From Liège to Aachen, extremely beautiful university buildings.

We looked about these universities in quest of a future haven of rest, in case the clerics in Berlin totally ruin even *Kupfergraben* for me. The Roman Curia would in any case be a more honorable opponent than the miserable and petty band of clerics in Berlin."[121]

In his course on Philosophy of World History (winter of 1826–1827), Hegel had lectured on the different religious conceptions of the doctrine of the sacrament, inveighing relentlessly against the dogma of transubstantiation. In order to prove how crude the Catholic ideas were and how crass their consequences could be, Hegel offered a rather peculiar argument: if a mouse devours the consecrated wafer, thereby containing in its body "the true body of the Lord," then a Catholic will have to kneel before the mouse and worship it.

The chaplain of St. Hedwig's Church, who regularly audited Hegel's courses, was present. After the incident, he complained to the Ministry of Education and Religion "about public slander of the Catholic religion," and thereby provoked ill feelings. When the chaplain showed up at Hegel's next lecture, the students booed him out of the auditorium.

On behalf of the Minister of Education, Dr. Schulze asked Hegel in strictest confidence to reply to the complaint. Hegel did so in a *letter of justification* (April 3, 1826) to the full satisfaction of the Ministry. This letter, omitted from the standard edition of Hegel's correspondence, was published by Haym:

"Privy Councilor Schulze's disclosures made to me in strictest confidence at the request of the Minister and concerning alleged remarks that I am said to have made about the Catholic religion in my lectures, oblige me to render the following statements, whose essential contents I already publicly addressed to my audience from my cathedra after being informed of the above-mentioned complaint:

a. That since I am a Professor of Philosophy at the Royal Prussian University of Berlin as well as a Lutheran Christian, nothing else can be expected of me than to speak in such capacity about the teachings and the spirit of Catholicism; that finding this to be unusual is rather novel; I would have to regard any other expectation as a personal insult, nay, an insult to the high government, which is not only tolerant toward the Protestant Chruch, but which for a long time now has had the sublime position of being at the head of the Protestant States in Germany and to which all Protestants constantly look and which they view as their chief support and mainstay. [. . .]

c. That in the interest of scholarship, which is my sole guidance in any lectures I give, I could not be content with mild and diffident, nor even condemnatory and dooming generalities, I had to view

Catholicism in its central point, the eucharist, and speak about it with scholarly precision, and thus discuss and proclaim Luther's doctrine as the true [religion] acknowledged as true by philosophy. I would, incidentally, be guilty of disrespect in this statement if I were to demand express assurance of my right as a Lutheran Christian to call the Catholic doctrine of the adoration of the host point-blank Papist idolatry and superstition. [. . .]

f. That, if a complaint is entered about statements that I made from the cathedra before Catholic spectators and that caused them offence, they must either complain against themselves for attending philosophical lectures given at a Protestant university by a professor who glories in having been baptized and brought up a Lutheran, who is and will remain one; or else they can blame their superiors who failed to warn them or, as was the case with the Catholic theology students, to forbid them to attend."[122]

Heinrich von Treitschke claims in his *German History of the Nineteenth Century:* "In his final years, [Hegel] was closely associated with the government and unscrupulously took advantage of Altenstein's and Johannes Schulze's goodwill in order to get rid of his scholarly rivals."[123] This description is unfair, however. Unless Treitschke drew on unnamed sources, his hard judgment can be based only on the "Beneke Affair"; no other case of this sort has come down to us. Eduard Beneke, a *privatdozent,* lost his right to teach *(venia legendi)* in 1822, "at Hegel's request and instigation." According to his own loyal pupil and follower, J. E. Erdmann, Hegel's conduct in this matter was such as to tarnish his memory.

There is no documentary evidence concerning this affair. But if one considers the bare facts only, then Hegel appears in a more favorable light. According to university regulations, the government was authorized to suspend or annul any revocable teaching permission if it deemed it necessary to do so. Since a dismissed instructor could not be hired at any other German university, a measure of this kind was a serious matter. Now Beneke had gotten his post-doctoral teaching degree in Berlin in 1820, at which time Hegel already was a faculty member. Beneke was dismissed for publishing *Foundation of a Physics in Ethics* and for including derogatory remarks about Hegel in his lectures. The report submitted to the government was signed by Hegel as well as Böckh and Bekker. Five years later Beneke regained his permission to teach from the same ministry and was fully rehabilitated. This happened in 1827, a time when Hegel's influence was greatest. Purely on the basis of these facts it must be said that even if Beneke's dismissal was due to Hegel, his rehabilitation could not have come about without Hegel's cooperation or at the very least his approval.[124]

The Household in Berlin

Let us now return to Hegel's private life and exchange official documents for something more artless: Hegel's budget book. On the first day of each quarter, he noted the receipt of 500 thalers salary minus 7 thalers and 20 groschen for the Widow's Fund. As for domestic expenses, Hegel regularly provided "my wife" with the necessary wherewithal; every week he entered the amount of money he gave her, payment of arrears, plus a round sum (10 thalers) for the next few days. He himself took care of the rent, the maid's salary, and the purchase of wine. The rent was rather high for those times: 300 thalers a year *postnumerando*. In addition to the rent, Hegel had to pay a quarterly sum of 1 thaler for garbage removal and a "service charge" of 1 thaler, 9 groschen, and 4 pfennigs. The maid received 7 thalers and 12 groschen quarterly; Hegel, paying her salary on February 6, conscientiously adds as a reproach for himself or his wife: "Should have been paid on New Year's Day." Relations between his family and the serving girl were evidently quite friendly; on July 11, while making some major purchase, Hegel had "borrowed 15 thalers from Anna," but was able to note the next day: "Paid Anna her 15 thalers back." The consumption of wine in the Hegel home was not trifling; in the first few months of the year, there are entries almost every other day concerning the purchase of several bottles of wine. Subsequently, he ordered wine by the quart and finally even in 50-quart barrels. In January, there were 19 bottles; in February, 17; in March, 4 bottles and 18 quarts; in April, 15 quarts and a 50-quart barrel. The average price per bottle was 18 groschen; at first, there is no mention of specific labels outside of Cahors, merely wine, red wine, and at one point Rhine wine. But then in May, there are 25 bottles of Madeira and 51 bottles of Haut Sauterne. For the rest of the year, things remain more or less the same, but naturally wine consumption is lower than during the "social season."

Hegel, as we know, greatly enjoyed socializing and took part with keen delight in the social life of Berlin. Among the formal parties he gave in his home, he records two of them because of the extra household money he gave his wife: one on February 9 and one before March 20. In early May, he mentions by name two guests at a gathering in his home: Krause and Zelter. On July 12, he lists a party which cost him 7 thalers.[125]

"A trait less characteristic of a superior philosopher than an easygoing Berliner was Hegel's habit of faithfully playing the National Lottery and renewing his ticket semi-annually in all four classes. . . . Donations to charity were evidently taken care of by Frau Hegel with the household money; among her husband's entries there occurs only [one example of charity] . . . a contribution of 1 thaler, plus the "yearly sum to Luther's descendants: two thalers."[126]

Any renowned university professor has to suffer the ordeal of being at the mercy of an education-starved public, and it was just such a public that existed in nineteenth-century Berlin. He has to "put on a show for every visitor and signalize his peculiarities in every conversation with any other party." He is left with the alternatives of total isolation or spreading himself thin with all comers. Solger, choosing the former, had developed a more than forbidding manner; but Hegel, in accordance with his affable nature, had opted for sociability. Or rather, he never really made a conscious decision—it happened willy-nilly—and it was precisely his ingenuousness that enchanted the Berliners. As a result, Hegel was simply "swamped." He had to find a job for one person or get a professorship for another "out of thin air." If someone claimed to be studying philosophy or at least intending to do so, Hegel, "exhibiting endless *bonhomie*" submitted to any demands put on him.

Hegel's disciple and biographer, Karl Rosenkranz, deserves our thanks for several colorful brushstrokes in the portrait of his master: "Furthermore, Berlin's social life still had a great deal of informality and candor about it:

> *Sitting, and sipping their tea,*
> *They talked of love a lot,*
> *The gentlemen were aesthetic,*
> *The ladies had tender hearts.*
> *(Heine)*

After the July revolution, this happy-go-lucky joie de vivre changed into a significant inner tension, a delineation of which does not belong in the present context. However, biting, caustic humor, a basic feature of the Berlin character, had undergone its first higher formation during the previous century in the encyclopedist society surrounding Frederick the Great, and was alive in Hegel's time, though still primarily in the form of a smiling face . . .

But Hegel was completely devoid of any archness, though all Berliners, down to the common folk, are normally characterized by this trait, often to a very charming degree; it was totally incompatible with his Swabian naiveté.

[He was] adored by his children and idolized by his wife, who, being 22 years his junior, was not merely attached to him in wifely affection, but looked up to him in a childlike way. Endowed with imperturbable courtesy, he did everything he could to make his guests feel at home. Conversation at meals was usually such that

Hegel in his study (lithograph by L. Sebbers, 1828).

each visitor could participate either actively or as a listener. He himself could not speak without external difficulty. His organ did not favor discourse; his language was neither fluent nor elegant; he still retained his Swabian dialect and always accompanied his words with gestures of his arms and hands. But if a listener could overlook these outer trappings, the refrain was generally so solid, sensible, or else strikingly witty, that even the form could not be criticized. During a game of cards, he was quite amicable, one might even say condescending to the other players, his humor remaining constant whether he won or lost; smiling wrath was so deliciously suitable to the charming philosopher whenever he reproached his whist partner for poor playing. He would employ certain standard phrases and expressions which for all their triviality acquired sense and meaning through him. He liked to tease good-naturedly the people he particularly cared for. Thus, Professor Gans, one of his favorites, was often the object of joking reprimands if he started to ramble on during a rubber and diverted attention from the game itself. 'Stop chattering and pay attention!,' Hegel would call out cheerfully scolding him. But if he won a rubber and his opponent had courtcards that were of no help now, Hegel would smile glee-fully and say, 'Give them up for lost!' Even now, those who heard him use this expression apply it in similar cases. . . .

But we should not limit ourselves to the friendly aspect of Hegel's social relationships; there was an unpleasant side as well; his cate-gorical ways, his stubbornness, his refractoriness, his 'tyranny,' as the Berliners used to put it. . . . Thus, even with Hegel, the cheerful surface of a varied epicureanism, the intimacy with close friends . . . had an earnest, frequently melancholy side, and Hegel's tena-cious and rigorous character would even clash with his friends. As for those people who simply contradicted him, he was hard as nails, and he would need to be in an excellent mood to persuade himself to associate with them personally. He was capable of power-ful anger and rage, and if he felt that hatred was in order, then he hated with a vengeance. He was equally terrible when rebuking someone. Any person he attacked would soon be all atremble, and at times he would treat some unsuspecting soul like a schoolboy, giving him such a dressing-down that both the victim and the other people present would be shocked and alarmed."[127]

Hotho on Hegel

A masterful portrait of Hegel was penned by another disciple, the art critic and professor of aesthetics, Heinrich Gustav Hotho in his *Preliminary Studies for Life and Art* (1835):

"It was at the beginning of my studies that I went to pay my respects to him one morning, entering his room timidly and yet full of confidence. He was sitting at a large desk and rummaging about impatiently in a disorderly, chaotic heap of books and papers. His body, prematurely aged, was bowed and yet full of primal endurance and energy; a gray-and-yellow dressing-gown, casual and loose, tumbled along the bent figure down to the floor; there was no visible trace of imposing height or of captivating grace; a touch of simple, old-fashioned, respectable integrity was the most evident thing in his whole demeanor. I will never forget the first impression his face made on me. His features were cadaverously sallow and flaccid; they reflected no destructive passion, but rather the entire past of constant, taciturn thinking that went on day and night; the torment of doubt, the ferment of unappeasable and tempestuous thought did not seem to have tortured or upset this mind that had been cogitating, seeking, and finding for forty years; only the restless urge to develop the early kernel of happily discovered truth, to make it richer and deeper, more rigorous and imperative, had furrowed the brow, the cheeks, the mouth. If his mind slumbered, his features seemed old and faded; but when his mind awoke it had to express its full earnestness regarding some great matter that could be content only with the hard work of consummate development, an earnestness occupied with and delving into this matter for a great length of time. How dignified the whole head was, how noble the nose, the high but curved forehead, the calm chin; the nobility of loyalty and thoroughgoing probity in both major and minor matters, the lucid awareness of having sought with all his might an ultimate satisfaction in truth alone were individually graven on all his features. I had expected a groping or inflaming conversation of a scholarly nature and was extremely surprised that the exact opposite took place. Having just returned from a trip through the Low Countries, the strange man could only render a prolix account of the cleanliness in the cities, the grace and the artificial fertility of the land, the green, expansive fields, the herds, the canals, the towering mills and comfortable highways, the art treasures and the agreeable though ceremonious way of life, so that within half an hour I felt as much at home in Holland as in his place.

But a few days later, when I went to his course, I could neither adjust to his manner of lecturing nor follow his train of thought. Tired out, fretful and with his head bent down, he sat there almost crouching, turning pages, and hunting back and forth, up and down, in the long notebooks, and lecturing all the while: his constant hawking and coughing impeded the flow of words, every single sentence stood out in isolation, emerging strenuously, piecemeal and jumbled; every word, every single syllable came forth with great reluctance, receiving a wondrously profound emphasis from the timbreless voice, with its broad Swabian intonation making everything sound as if it were of utmost importance. Yet his over-all appearance and presence commanded such deep respect, such profound realization of his worthiness, and attracted others through the naiveté of such overpowering earnestness, that despite all my discomfort and although I could grasp little enough of what he was saying, I was utterly spellbound. Within a short time, by dint of zeal and perseverance, I had grown accustomed to this external side of his lecturing, and instantly the intrinsic qualities became more and more apparent, interweaving with the aforementioned defects to form an integral texture, which contained in itself alone the measure of its perfection. . . .

The more ardently the ancient prophets struggled with their speech, the pithier and more vigorous the half-conquering, half-vanquished product of their internal struggle. Like them, he fought and won in ponderous conciseness. Totally immersed in the subject matter, he seemed to be developing it out of itself, for its own sake, and hardly at all from his own mind, for the audience; and yet it proceeded from him alone, and an almost paternal concern for lucidity mellowed the rigid earnestness, which could easily have deterred one from attending to such laborious ideas. He began falteringly, made an effort to continue, started all over again, paused once more, spoke, reflected; the precise word seemed to be permanently lacking, and then it struck safe and sure; it seemed ordinary, and yet it was inimitably proper, unusual and yet the only right one; the exact idea seemed to be just around the corner, and yet it had already been expressed unnoticeably and as perfectly as possible. Now, the audience had grasped the clear meaning of the sentence and longed to go on. In vain. The idea, instead of moving forward, revolved in similar words around the same point over and over again. Yet if a listener's flagging attention wandered, beclouded by wool-gathering, to return abruptly startled to the lecture after a few minutes, the listener suffered the penalty of completely losing the thread. For, quietly and prudently progressing through seemingly insignificant middle terms, some complete thought had limited itself to onesidedness, driven itself apart to differences, involved itself in contradictions, whose triumphant solution could be brought to reunification only by a great struggle of opposites. . . . Through what immeasurable depths was one's thinking led, in what endless antitheses torn apart; everything gained seemed to be constantly lost again and every effort seemed useless, for even the highest power of cognition seemed compelled to stop mutely at the limits of its scope. But in the abyss of the seemingly indecipherable, that powerful intellect was delving and working in magnificently self-assured ease and calm. It was only then that his voice arose, his eyes gleamed intensely across those gathered before him and shone in the quiet blaze of their conviction-filled brightness, while he, never at a loss for words, reached through all the depths and heights of the soul. Everything he spoke in those moments was so lucid and exhaustive, and of such simple truthfulness that everyone able to grasp it felt as if he himself had found it and thought it, and all previous approaches vanished so totally that there remained no memory of dreamy days in which the same ideas would not have led to the same cognition.

It was only in the most comprehensible parts that he became clumsy and tiresome. He twisted and turned, every feature showing his ill humor at toiling and moiling with these things, and yet, when he had brought the tedious business to an end, everything was so clear and complete, that in this point, too, one had to admire the highly vivid peculiarity. On the other hand, he moved about with the same masterly skill in the most unconcrete abstractions as in the most active profusion of phenomena. He was able to project himself into any position—even that of another person—to an extraordinary degree and to present that position in its entire scope. He seemed to be bound up in it as if it were a world unto itself, and only after filling in the entire picture did he expose the defects, the contradictions which made it collapse or lead over to other levels and forms. He succeeded entirely in depicting epochs, nations, events, and individuals in this fashion; because his insight, which penetrated more deeply than others, allowed him ubiquitously to recognize the organic; and even in old age the energy of his original approach lost none of its youthful strength or vigor. In these depictions his great vocabulary fairly bubbled over; he could never terminate a series of precise adjectives, and yet each was necessary, original, unexpected, and so solid and compact that the perfect whole, which the various motley features had formed together never to vanish again, forced itself upon the mind. It was impossible for anyone else to alter such a structure; the forms into which it had been poured for all time were far too solid."[128]

Estrangement from Schelling

Hegel had broken with Schelling long before his own call to Berlin. More accurately, there had been no real breach, only a gradual estrangement. The last bit of correspondence was a letter Schelling wrote from Munich on November 2, 1807, to Bamberg. Hegel had sent him a copy of the *Phenomenology of Mind,* and Schelling replied:

Schelling (drawing by Franz Kruger).

"I've only read the introduction. Inasmuch as you mention its polemical part, I would by any fair measure of my opinion of myself think too little of my own person to assume that these polemics refer to me. They may apply, as you said in your letter, to abuses and to the parrots, although your preface does not even make this distinction. You can well imagine how glad I would be to get rid of those people once and for all. Anything on which we have really dissimilar convictions or views could be easily discovered and resolved between us without any compromise; for after all, everything is reconcilable except for one thing. Thus I admit that I still don't understand your intention in opposing Notion *(Begriff)* and Conception *(Anschauung)*. By Notion, you can only mean what you and I have called Idea *(Idee)*, whose very nature consists in having one side which is Notion and one side which is Conception. . . .
I wish you the very best; write me again soon and think of me affectionately as your only sincere friend, Schelling." [129]
The tone may seem a bit irritable; it is also possible that Schelling was waiting for some elucidating comment from Hegel. Yet one thing is certain: this was no "letter of farewell," such as Schelling had written to Röschlaub, Marcus, or Paulus. His last letter to Fichte was an angry one, deliberately aiming at an open rupture. But his letter to Hegel revealed a different mood: "I wish you the very best;

write me again soon, and think of me affectionately as your only sincere friend, Schelling." These words sound conciliatory. But Hegel did not reply. He may have been waiting for a further letter from Schelling, for some utterance of appreciation for his book. But nothing of the sort ever came. And during the next twenty-two years, neither of them could make up his mind to resume their dialogue or recommence their old friendship. For a while, they sent each other regards through third parties, but nothing further.[130]

However, they did meet on a few occasions. In 1812, Schelling came to Nuremberg twice, the first time without visiting Hegel ("Schelling, as I heard afterwards, passed through with his wife, but stopped for only a few hours and didn't see anyone because of his rheumatism (!?)"); the second time, he was on an official trip and dropped in on Hegel anyway ("Schelling paid me a friendly visit; we did not touch on philosophica"). Then, three years later, Hegel went to Munich and had some contact with Schelling, although probably no warm reconciliation resulted, for Hegel saw more of Jacobi than anyone else, and Jacobi and Schelling were at daggers drawn. In a letter to Frommann (April 1816), Hegel wrote:

"This past autumn, I finally spent two weeks [in Munich]—fourteen delightful and agreeable days with the friends I have there: Niethammer, good old Jacobi, whom I love and esteem and who bears me great affection, Roth, and Schelling, et al."[131]

In the ensuing years, the antagonism became public knowledge. As of 1821, Schelling's lectures contained attacks against Hegel, with the criticism and polemics growing more mordant from year to year. In 1841, King Friedrich Wilhelm IV summoned Schelling to Berlin, asking him as Hegel's most prominent adversary to weed out "the dragon seed of Hegelianism."

In the last year of Hegel's life, the two men met unexpectedly and purely by chance in Karlsbad. Hegel, after arriving on September 3, 1829, had learned that Schelling was there, too. Schelling wrote to his wife about it:

"Just imagine, yesterday as I was sitting in my bath, I heard a somewhat unpleasant, semi-familiar voice asking for me. The stranger gave [the attendant] his name: it was Hegel, from Berlin. . . . In the afternoon, he came a second time, very eager and ever so friendly, as if nothing had occurred between us; however, since we haven't had any scholarly conversation, which I intend to steer clear of, and he happens to be a very intelligent person, I did spend two agreeable hours with him in the evening. I still haven't returned his visit; the *Golden Lion* is a bit too far for me."[132]

And Hegel wrote to his wife:

". . . last night . . . I met an old acquaintance—Schelling—who arrived here a few days ago, alone like myself, to take the waters, unlike myself. He happens to be very healthy and fit; his taking the *sprudel* is merely a preventive measure. Both of us are very glad [to have met] and feel like old, harmonious friends. This afternoon, we took a stroll, and then in a *kaffeehaus* we read the official news of the capture of Adrianople in the *Österreichischer Beobachter;* we spent the evening together; and thus my day's work concludes with these lines that I write to you and with my memory of you all. . . .

Sunday—Yesterday, I was initiated into the drinking of *sprudel.* I had lunch with Schelling, climbed the third Kreuzberg, and in the evening Frau von Wahl arrived and took lodgings in my mediocre hotel. . . ."133

He wrote to Daub: ". . . I spent five days in Karlsbad with Schelling in harmonious friendship." And Daub's astonished reply was: "I am overjoyed to the bottom of my soul that you and Schelling got along in the old harmonious way. The scribes and party disciples consider such a thing impossible."134

There is no use asking who was responsible for the antagonism, unless one cares to voice reproaches against either of the men, as has occurred in almost all biographies. The two friends were not separated by human antipathy, and ultimately no personal quarrel was the cause. But a dissimilarity of talent, disposition, and hence philosophy, aggravated as it was by sensitive vanity, led from objective difference to mutual personal rejection. The academic world witnesses the like at all times.

Birthday Celebration 1826

Hegel's stature in Berlin had grown from year to year. On his fifty-sixth birthday, August 27, 1826, his friends and his students wanted to make a public demonstration of their esteem for him. The occasion may not have been significant enough for such a celebration, but the devotion of those involved appears all the more convincing for it. A committee was formed consisting of some twenty members, including Förster as main speaker, Gans, Hotho, the land-scape artist Rösel, Zelter, the director of the Singing Academy, et al. Hegel's family did not attend the surprise party, since Frau Hegel and the children were visiting relatives in Nuremberg. But owing to this circumstance, we have a personal account by Hegel, who wrote to his wife on August 29, 1826:

"I have to tell you about my birthday. Your little gift, which Frau Aimée [von Hartwig] so charmingly prepared behind my back, and the letters from the boys delighted me so very much, and in my soul's eye I greeted you and kissed you very tenderly. Although Frau Aimée arose early and took great care to let me see your gift before anything else, she did not arise early enough. For we had already begun celebrating my birthday from its very first second at 12 midnight. I was at Herr Bloch's house, playing whist, a long and drawn-out game, and while we were having a protracted supper, the night watchman's whistle ushered in the twenty-seventh, and in response glasses clinked and drowned his whistle out; we—myself and everyone there—the Zelters were present too—drank mainly to your health—especially Rösel in his warm-hearted fashion.

In the morning, various well-wishers, good, dear souls and friends, plus several letters containing poems; then an official conference, during which I had a visitor—guess who—His Excellency Privy Councilor Von Kamptz in person. At lunch, I observed moderation and tenderly touched glasses and drank with you alone, at the proper time—saving myself for the evening. Great honors, joy, and demonstrations of love were awaiting me. In a new restaurant located on the *Unter den Linden*—which was celebrating its opening—a great dinner—so ample that it would deserve my describing it to you, like a complete and utterly exquisite banquet. Förster, the master of ceremonies, Gans, Hülsen, Hotho, Rösel, Zelter, and so on, some twenty people. Next came a deputation of students, handing me a costly silver goblet—(when the silver merchant heard that it was meant for me, he donated something of his own, since he had once attended my lectures)—on a velvet cushion plus a sheaf of poems—a great many more were recited—Rösel's, as well—he had sent me an antique gift that morning—in short, it was difficult to bring things to an end by midnight. It goes without saying that the students brought along music and trumpet flourishes. The company retained them, as it were, for the course of the meal. One of the guests was Professor Wichmann whom I didn't know. I was told that he had been commissioned to do a bust of me—which had been discussed for so long, and which Rauch hadn't been able to do. Next week—I still have to lecture this week—I'm going to sit for him. I would like to send my mother-in-law a copy. If you want it to be a surprise don't say anything to her. I could have surprised you, too, but you know that I don't really care for surprises—and I wanted to tell you about the love and honor that were mine on my birthday—(not to forget a flower vase of crystal from Herr von Hülsen)—and so at midnight we joined my birthday to Goethe's on the twenty-eighth.

Yesterday I slept until 11 a.m., and felt somewhat refreshed, not so much from physical fatigue—as from deeply moved feelings—(upon getting up, I received another poem, a matutinal greeting from Dr. Stieglitz). You won't believe what heartfelt and profound demonstrations of confidence, love, and esteem I received from my

Hegel (painting by Jack Schlesinger, c. 1825).

dear friends—mature and young. It was a rewarding day—rewarding for many efforts of my life.

Now I have to prevent too much of a good thing; if a circle of friends talks too much, although with good reason, it makes a different impression on the outside world."[135]

This line alludes to an article in the *Vossische Zeitung* which reported the birthday celebration. Varnhagen writes:

"Hegel's opponents raised a clamor about the August 27th celebration devoted to him and Goethe; they were particularly vexed by the description of the party in the *Vossische Zeitung;* the King, through a cabinet order, has enjoined the Supreme Censorship Office to make sure that such write-ups of private celebrations do not appear in the newspapers; it seems that it is not considered proper to treat anything but royal family parties and official celebrations with such importance. Philosophy, although still thought highly of by the government, ought to beware! The Court will manage to do it some mischief, and Hegel is no safer than anyone else."[136]

Hegel's Speeches as President of the University

Hegel was elected President of the University for the school year of 1829–1830. During his administration, he gave two public speeches in Latin: the first upon taking office on October 18, 1829;

the second, on June 25, 1830, on behalf of the Academic Senate
in honor of the tricentennial celebration of the *Augsburg Confession.*

In his inaugural address, Hegel—observing the conventional for-
malities and civilities of his time—urged the students to make
correct use of academic freedom, cautioning them against abuse
and license.

His jubilee speech was on *Christian Liberty as the Essence of Protestantism.* The *Augsburg Confession* of 1530 was the symbolic book of
the Lutherans, and it was often quoted against the Calvinists and
to prevent any unification with them. Now the Prussian government had—not without difficulty—made the union of Calvinists
and Lutherans the principle of ecclesiastical development in Prussia. Thus, Hegel's task was a rather delicate one. His skillful way of
extricating himself is described by Rosenkranz:

"Despite his deep-seated Lutheran fervor, a product of his up-
bringing, Hegel's speech avoided anything that might have stressed
Lutheranism in particular or discredited ever so slightly either the
profession of faith or the ecclesiastical constitution of the Reformed
Church. . . .

On the other hand, he laid great emphasis on the relationship
of the Reformation to Romanism. And, in opposition to [Romanist]
sanctimonious Pelagianism, he extolled the *Augsburg Confession* because of its *sola fides justificat* as the *Magna Carta* of *Protestantism.* He
described the corruption of the church due to *papist* Catholicism in
the fifteenth and the sixteenth century, and the tyranny with which
the church had stifled all independent science and scholarship and
curtailed freedom of religion. He described the corruption of life
through: *the destruction of conscience and responsibility* due to an obtuse,
immature obedience, which in its lack of independent thinking left
all responsibility for its actions to the priests; and finally, the destruction of civil government, not only by scorn and condemnation of
marriage, private property, and intellectual self-assurance, but also
by the refusal to acknowledge the sovereignty of the ruler. In contrast, he enthusiastically praised Protestantism as the restorer of the
morals of family life, civic integrity, conscience and freedom of
conscience, unity of God and man, as particularly expressed in the
fact that the *ruler* of a Protestant State was simultaneously the
Supreme Bishop of its church."[137]

Last Political Work

Hegel's last piece of political writing is his essay *On the English
Reform Bill,* two-thirds of which was serialized in four successive
issues (Nos. 115–118) of the *Allgemeine Preussische Staatszeitung.* The
final part was printed and distributed secretly, since the highest

authorities had misgivings about letting a ministerial paper publish such critical remarks as Hegel's on conditions in England. He attacked primarily the weakness of the royalist principle against Parliament, the garrulity of political declamation, the peculiarity of English civil law, and—here his anger mounted—the cruel treatment of Ireland. Exhibiting an amazing knowledge of details, Hegel opposed both blind admiration of England and blind contempt of Germany on a political level. Hegel, as he says himself, was enraged by the Reform Bill and its presentation in Parliament, because he saw in it "a deviation from England's principle, an evasion of strictly positive law." Day and night, he was beset by worry and haunted by tormenting images.

In the summer of 1831, his political fury was interrupted by another vexation. Coming from the east, a cholera epidemic broke out in Germany, spreading rapidly, especially in Berlin. Hegel had reached the end of the summer semester without mishap, and together with his family he retired to the upper story of a belvedere, the so-called "little castle" in Grunow Garden in Kreuzberg, Berlin. Few friends attended his birthday party, most of them having left the city because of the epidemic. Rösel's fine sense of humor is evident in this account of a cheerful dinner in one of the spacious halls of the Tivoli gardens near by:

"Zelter inexhaustibly repeated interesting comments and bons mots of Goethe's. The painter Zeller made use of his Swabian good-naturedness and his fetching smile to season the enjoyment of jokes that were made; Marheineke emanated a beneficent dignity whose ironical tolerance encouraged the joviality; Hegel's sons sympathized with the ladies in glad and quiet emotion. No sooner had we finished our coffee after the champagne, than a terrible storm gathered, inducing most of the guests to leave quickly; Hegel, too, hurried to his house near by." [138]

With the approach of late autumn and the new semester, the epidemic began to subside. Hegel and his family returned to their home on *Kupfergraben*. For the winter term, he had announced two lecture courses: *Philosophy of Law,* from 12 to 1, and *History of Philosophy,* from 5 to 6. At the time, an awkward incident had greatly vexed Hegel. Gans, his dearly beloved pupil, friend, and colleague (and his junior by a whole generation), had placed a notice on the University bulletin board, advising students of law to attend Hegel's "very useful" course on the philosophy of law. Hegel regarded this as tutelage, which he felt he did not need in the least. In a fierce and irate letter to Gans he demanded that the notice be removed immediately, since it was compromising him with both the teachers, the students, and his colleagues. Hegel added that he couldn't see why anyone would dare to recommend him, and he was willing to forget the matter out of friendly consideration.

Aside from a few instructions sent to a printer's office, these were Hegel's last written words. Feeling perfectly well, he had given his first lecture on Thursday, November 10, and continued the following morning. His students recalled that he had spoken with unusual zeal and ardor. Upon coming home, he was still in a good mood, and said to his wife: "I had a particularly easy time of it today."

Illness, Death, Funeral

To everyone's amazement, Hegel died, on November 14, 1831, "of cholera in its concentrated form, the external symptoms of which are less terrible." The diagnosis of "cholera sicca" was instantly queried and, according to Glockner's thorough investigations, cannot be maintained. The more likely cause of death was an acute exacerbation of a chronic stomach ailment, which had become noticeable during Hegel's trip to Paris in 1827, and from which he had never really recovered. In the summer of 1830, he was bedridden for three months, suffered frequent attacks of indigestion, and had to limit his diet to "nourishing soups and light meat dishes." Minor physical exertions wore him out; wind and sudden changes in the weather were much harder on him than ever before. His increasing weakness was accompanied by mental depressions. To his wife's astonishment, Hegel, who was usually cheerful, became inexplicably dejected, unhappy, and pessimistic, a state that could alter just as quickly. Obviously, his death came as a surprise only to outsiders. If the terrors of cholera had not been on the rampage, no doctor would have ever come up with the diagnosis of "cholera sicca." A letter from Frau Hegel to her sister-in-law Christiane contains a reliable and detailed account of Hegel's last days, his dying, and his funeral:

"I'll pull myself together and tell you briefly how everything came about. Starting Sunday morning, my late beloved husband, after breakfasting with us in high spirits, felt ill and complained of a stomach-ache and nausea, although *he had not broken his diet or caught cold.* On the previous Thursday, he had begun his lectures in full vigor and of good cheer; on Saturday, he had given an oral examination; and for Sunday, he had invited a few dear friends to dinner. I let them know what had happened and devoted myself entirely to nursing him. By a fortunate coincidence, the physician came instantly, prescribed—but none of us saw anything to worry about in his condition. His stomach pains were bearable. It was only after a while that he began vomiting gall. He had suffered such attacks often. He spent an extremely restless night. I sat at his bedside, tucking him in whenever he sat up or tossed about, although he asked me over and over again and in the friendliest of tones to lie down and leave him to his impatience. His gastric pains were not so violent, 'but past remedy like a toothache, you couldn't remain lying in the same position.' On Monday morning he wanted to get up. We took him into the adjacent room, but he was so weak that on the way to the sofa he nearly collapsed. I had his bed brought over next to it. After thoroughly warming the bedclothes, we put him to bed. He complained only about feeling weak. All his pains, his nausea were gone, so that he said: 'If God had only granted me just one such peaceful hour last night.' He said he needed rest and told me not to receive any visitors. Whenever I wanted to feel his pulse, he tenderly clasped my hand as if to say, don't worry about it. The doctor came early in the morning, prescribing (as on the day before) a mustard plaster on the abdomen (the previous evening I had applied leeches). Later in the morning, he began hiccuping and had difficulty urinating. But all the same, he rested quite calmly, staying evenly warm and sweating, and completely conscious, and—it seemed to me—without any thought of danger. A second physician, Dr. Horn, was summoned: mustard plasters for the entire body, covered by flannel cloths soaked in camomile extract. None of this bothered or worried him. At three o'clock he had cramps in his chest, followed by a peaceful sleep; but an icy cold drew across the left half of his face. His hands became blue and cool. We knelt down at his bed and listened to his respiration. It was the slumber of a sainted man resigning his breath!

Let me stop. Now you know everything. Weep with me, but let us thank God for a painless, peaceful, Christian death. And now tell me, would you have recognized even *one* symptom of cholera in all this? Terrified, I had to learn that both physicians, Medical Councilor Barez and Privy Councilor Horn, had made that diagnosis, recognizing a form of cholera that, without external symptoms, violently destroys the interior. I did not see his interior at all.

Even though Hegel was reported as a case of intercurrent cholera (the [Medical] Commission allowed me to keep the beloved body in my living room, and fumigated and disinfected everything), none of our friends, not even the most apprehensive, were afraid. All of them, in their grief, hurried to my side. Some of them had seen him during the past few days in the best of health, had attended his Thursday and Friday classes, at which he had enraptured his audience with unusual energy and ardor, so that he had even told me: 'I had a particularly easy time of it today.' Many [of our friends] could barely regain their self-possession. During his

Phillip Konrad Marheineke (portrait sketch by Franz Krüger).

illness, which lasted from 11 o'clock on Sunday to 5 o'clock on Monday, none of his dearest friends had even the remotest idea. No one saw him again except Privy Councilor Schulze, whom I, in my extreme anguish, had sent for to be present at [Hegel's] death. His heavenly repose and his Christian death were undisturbed by any visible disquiet or blatant moaning. Containing our tears and with heavy hearts, we remained silent and quiet, trying to appear as calm as possible, devoting ourselves to him until we listened to his last sleep, in which we were unable to make out his decease. We could only fall to our knees and pray.

Through the more than active mediation of our friends, a first and only exception was granted out of respect for the importance of the sainted man, after unspeakable struggles and higher intercession: he did not have to be carried on the wagon for cholera victims, within twenty-four hours, in the middle of the night, to the cholera cemetery. He is buried in the place he picked out at Solger's funeral and called his own—next to Fichte and near Solger [in the *Dorotheenstadter Friedhof* at *Oranienburger Tor,* Berlin]. Yesterday, Wednesday, at three in the afternoon, the funeral procession took place. Professors and students from all faculties, his older and younger disciples, gathered beforehand in the main hall of the university. Here, his faithful friend Marheineke, now President of the University, gave a speech to the deeply agitated audience. Then the immeasurably long cortege of students got underway; not being allowed to accompany him with blazing torches, the students wreathed crepe about them; an endless line of carriages followed them to the house of mourning, where they joined the funeral coach drawn by four horses. My poor sons, who were dreadfully shaken, drove along behind the beloved body, together with Marheineke and Privy Councilor Schulze. Upon reaching the city gate, the students began to sing a chorus. At the grave, Aulic Councilor Förster delivered an address; Marheineke, being a clergyman, spoke the benediction."[139]

8

The Hegelian Schools

Opponents and Followers

Hegel had died peacefully and at the height of his fame; unlike Schelling he never became a has-been. It is easy to claim that after Hegel's death German philosophical classicism collapsed and that philosophy declined into the lows of positivism and materialism, rising again only after 1871. For a while, Hegel's pupils were given preference in regard to teaching positions. His philosophy was taught at most German universities, and in the sharp antithesis of his opponents, he remained the violently controversial and yet undeniable sovereign of nineteenth-century philosophy.

But for Berlin, "the philosophical epoch" came to an end shortly after Hegel's death. Rudolf Virchow, in a speech he gave as University President (August 3, 1893) described "the transition from the age of philosophy to the age of natural science" in regard to Hegel:

". . . in 1818, Berlin gained the quick-witted dialectician. Everyone eagerly looked forward to his lectures. His circle of followers grew rapidly, increasing from year to year. Soon his influence on the thought and speech of his contemporaries was so great that Hegelians were to be found on every faculty. They totally revised all scholarship and brought the Master's terminology into the farthest depths of every special discipline. When cholera, taking its first toll throughout our country, carried him off on November 14, 1831, he left behind a veritable general staff of trained disciples, who set themselves the task of continuing his work and handing down to future generations the tradition of his ideas. Nothing seemed more solidly constructed than this school. Theology and law, political science and aesthetics were transcribed into Hegelian language and mentality; it was only in medicine and the natural sciences that the invasion was limited to a few advocates. Although the Master was gone, his aura survived for a whole decade—one can say until the death of King Friedrich Wilhelm III—thanks preeminently to the benevolence of *Kultusminister* Altenstein, himself an enthusiastic Hegelian. But none of Hegel's disciples had the creative initiative or even the enthusiasm to sway large groups of people: their frequently pedantic and sterile phrase-mongering, a residue of the movement, ultimately became an object of ridicule, just as earlier it had been the object of awe and admiration.

For King Friedrich Wilhelm III, Hegelianism was the last in the series of philosophical schools which he had personally witnessed in succession. He had never gotten too familiar with the philosophy of nature in its more rigorous, or better, more consistent execution. Its advocate, Schelling, first Fichte's disciple, then his opponent, then his successor in Jena, had soon moved to Bavaria, and here his bold incursions into physiology and pathology managed to draw the attention of medical men to himself and his ideas. But the leading position which the philosophy of nature actually managed to attain in medicine did not last long; in Berlin, this doctrine would have passed without leaving a single trace if Hegel had not incorporated in his own system a number of his friend Schelling's ideas.

Strangely enough, a few decades after the actual flowering of natural philosophy, ten years after Hegel's death, right after the demise of King Friedrich Wilhelm III, an unexpected turn of events took place, and the philosophy of nature seemed to be on the point of occupying a vacant Chair. Friedrich Wilhelm IV, not long after his accession to the throne, offered Schelling a professorship at the University of Berlin [1841]. There were not enough auditoriums to hold the massive audience, which consisted of both students and numerous representatives from all the educated strata, who wanted to hear the (almost divine) revelations from the famous philosopher's own lips. His auditors soon realized something they might have known anyway: to wit, that the aging philosopher was trying to cover up the defects in his doctrine with all kinds of mystical supplements and a confusing phraseology, and yet had not advanced further or more deeply in his thinking. Consequently, the experiment was soon terminated, and natural philosophy together with its author vanished from Berlin, where Hegelianism had prepared the soil and yet exhausted it as well. . . .

One thing is certain in any case: with Hegel's death, the university forever broke the spell binding it to philosophical systems. Since then, no philosopher has played such a dominating role or even (and we may voice our gratitude) laid claim to one. However, if we wish to sum up the reign of Friedrich Wilhelm III, nothing could define it more precisely than to label it the philosophical era." [140]

In a certain sense, Hegel's death marked a standstill, although not in the way he had himself pictured such a standstill, that is, that the history of philosophy would raise all earlier antitheses to a higher unity and that his system would conclude all previous philosophical development. The stagnation was in part really more of a lull preceding a storm inasmuch as the multifarious political and social conflicts of the day were lying just below the surface; and on the other hand, the gradual advances of the other disciplines checked the domination of philosophy. The opponents of Hegelianism divided—according to Hegel's principle of dialectics—into an antithetical opposition; and the same may be said of Hegel's disciples: they split into "rightwing and leftwing Hegelianism," these labels being based on a suggestion of D. F. Strauss's (to be discussed below). The "Historical School"—as represented by Hegel's colleague, Savigny, Professor of Roman Law at Berlin, and the historian Ranke—protested against Hegel's interpreting all historical events as mere transitional stages in a dialectical world-process. Herder had made a principle of the intrinsic value of all nations and incorporated the results of his research as a task of the romantic trend. Hegel's teleological world history and his influence on historiography in terms of intellectual history was opposed by the growth of a positive study of history founded on fact. These investigations of historical facts were accompanied by the development of an exact natural science, which was highly scornful of Hegel's metaphysical and religious speculations.

The "Right Wing" and the "Left Wing"

Within the Hegelian schools, the conservatives formed a right wing (including Carové, Erdmann, K. Fischer, Gans, Hinrichs, Michelet, Oppenheim, Rosenkranz, and Rössler) and defended the privilege of historical tradition in politics, philosophy, and theology. The left wing revindicated Hegel's dialectical method, turning it into a revolutionary principle. [141]

It would be a good idea to say a word about the term school, the use of which is apparently taken for granted. Very few philosophical systems have led to the crystallization of schools. A plethora of followers does not necessarily form a close union. That is to say, a "school" doesn't have to be a unified organization. A teacher and an authoritative doctrine are essential and indispensable, however, as are joint work by the adherents in some geographically fixed place, unity without uniformity, and a basis for passing on the tradition. In this sense, neither Kant, Fichte, nor Schelling had founded a school. However great Kant's influence may have been, initiating as it did a new era in philosophy, the term "Kantianism" refers to a viewpoint of principles and methods, but not a "school." Hegel's system and his personality, on the other hand, were more readily disposed to starting a philosophical school. But from the very first, the dialectical double aspect of his ideology ripped apart the unity (if ever any was sought) and militated against the formation of a solid and compact school. Thus, in a narrow sense, there is no such thing as a "Hegelian School," but rather only a school-like reliance on the Master's authority.

Philosophical histories usually trace the influence of Hegel on the left wing, including such figures as Ludwig Feuerbach, Bruno Bauer, Friedrich Engels, and Karl Marx. As Hermann Lübbe says:

"Marx, compared with the right wing Hegelians, is certainly the only Hegelian of any historical and international importance. Yet in the nineteenth century, no one realized this. Not because no

Hegel's grave.

other genius was great enough to recognize Marx's genius. Marx owes his historical and international success not so much to the correctness of his analyses and prognoses as to his formulating a political will, which in its fantastic abstractness had little effect in the time and place of its own intentions (the West European industrial countries in their early phase of capitalism), but which was fortunate enough later and elsewhere to encounter and ignite the dormant political energy of a bankrupt and relatively backward state. It is this success alone that makes an intensive study of Marx both a necessity and a requirement. In the context of the history of nineteenth-century ideologies, Marx's role is not different from the part he actually played in the consciousness of his contemporaries, who could not possibly foresee his later triumph. . . . In relation to [the left wing], the right wing of the Hegelian school remained realists. Their political inclinations, in Hegel's wake, developed in terms of, even anxiously close to, reality and, rather than Marx's international proletarian revolution, they planned at best tax-free sugar and coffee for the working classes. This concretism, this inability of the political will to advance to complete opposition to the status quo, is one of the decisive effects wrought by Hegel through his school on the nineteenth century. . . . This right wing Hegelianism of the school exerted a greater influence on the nineteenth century than left wing radicalism. In the element of philosophy it represents the politically liberal mentality of a middle class educated in German classicism—the world of, say, Varnhagen, who may be considered a supreme representative of the audience that responded to Hegelian philosophy. All in all, we have to conclude that right wing Hegelianism is more an articulation than an effective political power. Although revealing the things that existed, it never brought forth any new movement or reality. And this is where it confirms itself to be true Hegelianism, insofar as Hegel himself, claiming that it was the function of philosophy to be the spirit of the age in ideas, assigned [philosophy] the role of representation rather than action."[142]

In the 1830's, no problem stirred up the minds of Hegel's friends and adversaries so much as that of the relationship between philosophy and Christian religion and theology. The stance of Hegelian philosophy on dogma constituted the theme of criticism. After K. F. Göschel, in his *Aphorisms on Ignorance,* tried to reconcile the standpoint of religious faith with Hegel's theses, others attempted to interpret Hegel's ideas in terms of orthodox Christianity, and further scholars, for example, Rosenkranz, wanted to at least bridge the antithetical gap between Hegel and Schleiermacher. Even the radical persuasion joined the battle.

David Friedrich Strauss

The antitheses were fully revealed when the theologian, David Friedrich Strauss, published his work, *The Life of Jesus,* in 1835. Strauss, coming to Berlin in the winter of 1831–1832, had managed to attend Hegel's first few lectures at the start of the semester and immediately made friends with two of Hegel's pupils, Michelet and Vatke. Shortly thereafter, he became a preceptor in Tübingen, where Ferdinand Christian Baur, the leader of the Tübingen school of critical history, was teaching. Strauss's book unleashed a whirlwind of controversy in Germany. Strauss had called all rationalistic and supra-rationalistic Biblical exegeses erroneous and interpreted New Testament texts on Jesus as myths. This was a declaration of war against both Christian dynamics and the speculation of several of Hegel's disciples. The keen dispute, manifested in countless critical reviews, raged within the Hegelian school as well. Strauss's rejoinder was his *Pamphlet of Defense* (1837), which explicitly stated that from the very first his criticism of the life of Jesus was intrinsically related to Hegel's philosophy. His most significant adaptation was to incorporate in theological discourse Hegel's distinction between Image [*Vorstellung*] and Notion [*Begriff*], which despite different forms can have identical substance.

Strauss claimed that anyone contradicting him on this point—as Marheineke and Göschel had done—was merely confirming "that in theology, the Hegelian School had relapsed from Hegel's position into Schelling's." Strauss detected some uncertainty in Hegel's views on the personality and the life of Jesus. Concerning the question of whether and to what extent the idea of the unity of divine and of human nature posits the historical factualness of the Gospel accounts, Strauss feels there are three possible answers: with that concept of unity, the New Testament can be proved to be historical (1) in its entirety, (2) in part, or (3) not at all. If each of these answers represented the position of a separate branch of the Hegelian School, then Strauss proposes that one could distinguish between a right wing, a center, and a left wing. The subsequent division between Hegelian rightists and leftists is derived from this suggestion, though Strauss made it only hypothetically and in reference to a specific problem. The primary advocates of the far right were, according to Strauss, Göschel, and Gabler. Bruno Bauer is still right of, but closer to, the center, believing as he does that the miracles of Jesus can be conceptually deduced. Rosenkranz is a middle-of-the-roader, because he acknowledges contradictions in the history of Jesus and considers some of the miracles incomprehensible, but nevertheless feels that "the essence of the idea includes in itself the absoluteness of the phenomenon as a microcosm." But Strauss places himself at the extreme left with his opinion that it is wholly up to historical criticism to test the truth of Biblical accounts. Strauss was not interested in classifying the trends inside the Hegelian school; he merely wanted to clarify their various views on the question of Christology. Michelet, in general agreement with Strauss, proposed a coalition of the center with the left wing, claiming that Hegel himself would have approved, since—despite Strauss's comment—the Master's ideas did not suffer from uncertainty.[143]

Julius Schaller, in his book, *Philosophy of Our Time* (1837), attacked Hegelianism for deteriorating into formalism and dogmatism, teaching a system of necessity in lieu of freedom and denying the personality of God. And the historian, Heinrich Leo, severely condemned "the young Hegelian party." Leo had usually been on the best of terms with Hegel and had called him his "most cherished teacher" when Hegel was to intercede on his behalf after Leo had become publicly involved in a jealousy scandal and had resigned his professorship. Leo's book, *The Junior Hegels (Die Hegelingen)* (1838), was a severe settling of accounts. He openly accused the Hegelian party of professing a religion of this world, preaching atheism, labeling the gospel a mythology, and yet—"by disguising ungodly and blasphemous teachings in a repugnant and abstruse phraseology"—giving itself the reputation of being a Christian party. The greatest danger, according to Leo, consisted in the fact that the junior Hegelians did not so much want to propound mere theories as to exert an influence on life.

The Halle Yearbooks *and Ludwig Feuerbach*

The university lecturer, Arnold Ruge, a violent opponent of Leo, joined forces with Theodor Echtermeyer in 1838 to put out the *Halle Yearbooks for German Learning and Art*. The staff of this Hegelian literary organ, which lasted for three years, included Strauss, Feuerbach, Vatke, Bruno and Edgar Bauer, the philosopher of aesthetics, Vischer, and others. At first, by closely following Hegel's teachings, they tried to outwardly demonstrate the unity of the school. Gradually, criticism of Hegelian philosophy became more and more vehement. The right wing of the school had to endure ridicule and total rejection; politically, the times favored a struggle against prevailing conditions, especially those in the Prussian State. Romanticism was called the "sphere of the dim medium": its father was Fichte, its mother Schelling, whose theories were an "apostasy from philosophy," whereas Hegelian philosophy overcame romanticism only by means of negation.

In 1841, the *Halle Yearbooks* were transformed into the *German*

Yearbooks. The practical and political tendency became more and more pronounced, while the philosophical one lost ground. After the periodical was banned in Saxony (1843), Ruge betook himself to France. In 1844, the *German-French Yearbooks* appeared, edited by Ruge and Karl Marx. This periodical began a new phase in the development of Hegelianism, a phrase which will have to be gone into further.[144]

In 1839, Ludwig Feuerbach published (in the *Halle Yearbooks*) a *Critique of Hegelian Philosophy,* in which he renounced Hegel's "rational mysticism" and demanded a philosophy of the reality of individuality and nature. In his magnum opus, *The Essence of Christianity* (1841), he cast off "all metaphysics" and spurned "absolute, immaterial, self-satisfied speculation—speculation which draws its substance out of itself." The principle of his own philosophy was not to be the absolute spirit, but man, "the flesh-and-blood result of all previous philosophy." Feuerbach regarded his ideas as necessary progress, through which the truth of Hegelian philosophy comes to the fore and goes through *Aufhebung.*

Feuerbach took the cardinal sentence in Hegel's philosophy of religion ("Man knows about God only insofar as God knows about himself within man; this knowledge is God's self-awareness as well as God's knowledge of men, and this knowledge that God has of men is man's knowledge of God; man's spirit in knowing God is merely God's spirit itself.") and reversed it, interpreting it in the following way: "If, as Hegel theorizes, man's awareness of God is God's self-awareness, then human awareness must per se be divine awareness," that is, "man's knowledge of God is man's knowledge of himself, his own essence." He therefore concludes that God's essence is in the same place as God's awareness—in man. "In God's essence, only your own essence becomes your object, and only that emerges into your awareness which resides behind your awareness." Thus, theology is completely absorbed in philosophical anthropology. In his *Lectures on the Essence of Religion,* Feuerbach is even more articulate: he wants to free man from the illusion of God, restore his full freedom, and make him a true human being. "The purpose of my writings and of my lectures is: to change men from theologians into anthropologists, from lovers of God into lovers of humanity, from candidates for the afterlife into students of the here and now, from religious and political valets of divine and worldly monarchy and aristocracy into free, self-confident citizens of the earth." And at the end of his last lecture, Feuerbach expresses the hope that he has not failed in his mission: "the mission of turning [men] from friends of God into friends of mankind, from believers into thinkers, from pray-ers into workers ... . from Christians—who according

to their own profession and admission are half-angel, half-animal—
into men, into whole men." [145]

Feuerbach goes on to say that Hegelian philosophy has estranged
man from himself, because its entire system is based on acts of
abstraction. Hegelianism may re-identify the things it separates,
but only in a re-separable, indirect way. The immediate identifica-
tion of man's essence, alienated by abstraction, with man himself
can be understood only as a total negation of Hegel's philosophy.
"Hegelian philosophy may contain everything, but always together
with its negation, its antithesis." Hence, true philosophy—if Hegel
is to be correctly interpreted—has to begin with non-philosophy,
that is, with life, with man. Truth can be found not so much in
thought as in the totality of human life. Anthropology thus becomes
the universal science. [146]

Yet Feuerbach's anthropologism can go to the extreme of radical
subjectivism and egoism as shown in Karl Stirner's *The Individual
and his Property* (1844). Stirner claims that Feuerbach's views are
perfectly theological. When Feuerbach says, "Man is, for man, the
highest being," we have to ask: "What do we gain when we take
the divine that is external to us, and for a change, shift it into
ourselves?" The Hegelian leftists have abolished the transcendental
and attained atheism, with only one man remaining; but a basic
error is involved: man's being raised to the divine. Stirner proposes
rather that "the divine is God's concern, and the human is man's
concern. My concern is neither the divine nor the human, nor the
True, the Good, the Right, the Free, etc.; my concern is only that
which is mine, and this is no universal concern, but individual, as
I am individual. . . . It is *my* being, just as that is *my* thinking." [147]

The 1850's marked the triumph of the empirical natural sciences,
which brought in their wake several kinds of materialism as philosophical doctrine. Hegel's constructions, particularly his philosophy
of nature—the weakest part of his system—were laughed to scorn.
But the Hegelians did not give up the fight. The Philosophical
Society of Berlin started a new periodical in 1860: *Der Gedanke* (The
Thought). That same year, the Herbartians had founded a *Journal
for Exact Philosophy*. The two magazines advocated respectively Hegel's
and Herbart's philosophy. The program of *Der Gedanke* (in the first
issue) states that the Herbartians believe they can turn back the
history of philosophy and brand "Kant, Fichte, Schelling, and Hegel
as excessive aberrations and destructive hair-splitters" in order to gain
"ground for their heroes." The Hegelians proudly pointed out that
Hegel's philosophy, "leaving Germany aside, had numerous followers
in Scandinavia, Russia, Poland, Serbia, Italy, and France and beyond
the Atlantic Ocean."

The magazine, which lasted until 1884, never managed to create a new position of power for Hegel's philosophy; however, it did testify to the survival of his ideas. Even after the Hegelian school had lost its one-time status, there were still enough Hegelians left to carry Hegelian philosophy into the twentieth century. In 1870, the centennial of Hegel's birth, a whole array of tributes appeared, including Michelet's *Hegel, the Unrefuted World Philosopher,* Rosenkranz's *Hegel as a German National Philosopher,* and Köstlin's *Hegel's Philosophical, Political, and National Significance.* Between the turn of the century and World War I, there was talk of a Hegel renaissance. In 1910, Wilhelm Windelband gave a speech on *The Renewal of Hegelianism.* Even today, Hegel's philosophy is taught at universities. Without attempting comprehensiveness, we can list the names of some of the men who have taught, interpreted, or edited Hegel's works: in Germany (besides those we have already mentioned), Adolf and Georg Lasson, Julius Ebbinghaus, Emil Hammacher, Theodor Litt, Johannes Hoffmeister, and Hermann Glockner; in France, Cousin, Ott, and Prevost; in Italy, Vera, Spaventa, Marino, d'Ercole, Croce, and Gentile; in England, Stirling, Green, Wallace, Seth, Edward and John Caird, Bosanquet, McTaggart, and Baillie; in Sweden, Höijer and Borelius; in Norway, Monrad; in Denmark, Heiberg; in Holland, Van Ghert and Bolland.[148]

9

Hegel and Marxism

Marx and Engels

Dialectical and historical materialism together form—in Soviet terminology—the "philosophy of communism," which in turn combined with political economy and political ideas make up the total system of Marxist-Leninist ideology. The triad was classically formulated by Lenin: "Marx's doctrine . . . is the legal heir of the best that mankind created in the nineteenth century in the form of German philosophy, English political economy, and French socialism."[149] This statement is worthy of note in our present context: Communist ideology views itself as the heir of German classical philosophy. It regards this fact as its superiority over mechanical materialism, which it often disparagingly labels "vulgar materialism."[150]

Soviet philosophy cites Marx and Engels as its real founders. In view of the circumstance that today nearly one billion people live in regimes based on Karl Marx's teachings, the importance of Marxism at first glance seems to have worldwide scope, and yet it is a product of German philosophy. Farsighted contemporaries of Marx pointed out that school philosophy, precisely thought out and eschewing all commotion, would some day climb down from academic cathedras into the political arena, causing enormous revolutionary changes. Naturally, we have no right to assume that everything happening in the Marxist world can be traced back directly to Marx. After all, certain events and changes cannot be completely

Hegel (lithograph by C. Mittag, 1842).

Karl Marx.

derived from the original doctrine. And yet they are somehow connected with it, either as deviations from Marxism or contradictions
to it.[151]

Karl Marx came to Berlin from Bonn as a young man in 1836
and attended Savigny's and Gans's lectures. Within a short time,
he joined the *Doktorklub* of Young Hegelians, and there he met
Köppen and Bruno Bauer. In 1837, the nineteen-year-old Marx wrote
to his father, "I had read fragments of Hegelian philosophy, but
didn't much care for their grotesque, craggy melody. Now I wanted
to dive into the sea again, but with the definite aim of finding
intellectual nature as necessary, concrete, and solidly rounded as
physical nature; of no longer practicing skillful feints, but holding
the pure pearl up to the sunlight instead." He tried in vain to
escape the transcendence of the Idea, to which philosophy, his "evil
spirit," led him:

"I wrote a dialog of some 24 folios: *Kleanthe or On the Starting
Point and the Necessary Progress of Philosophy*. It united to a certain
extent art and knowledge, which had moved far apart; and I, a
sturdy wanderer, went straight to work, attempting a philosophical-
dialectical development of the godhead, as it manifests itself as a

concept, as religion, as nature, as history. My final sentence was the beginning of the Hegelian system, and this paper, for which I did some delving into natural science, Schelling, and history, and which required endless cerebral effort and is written so chaotically [since it was actually meant to be a new logic], that even I can't think my way back into it—this dearest child of mine, fostered in moonlight, carries me like a treacherous siren into the enemy's arms."[152]

For a while, Marx turned to "more positive studies," but soon, during an illness, he re-read Hegel, and then his critical analysis of Hegel's philosophy began, concluding in 1845.

The Reversal of Hegel

Today, especially in the Western world, people speak of "Marxist materialism" or even "materialist Marxism," oblivious of the fact that Marx himself, emulating Feuerbach, used the term "materialism" simply in the sense of a reversal of Hegelian "idealism." Even the "reversal" is often extremely simplified, as if Marx had made out the ideal and the mind to be evolutionary products of matter, whereas Hegel had regarded nature and the material as the results of alienation. In point of fact, Marx's reversal of Hegel consisted in the following: "In the dialectical process of the self-realization of the absolute on the path of its self-alienation, it is not the Idea that appears as the subject, but rather Nature together with the sensible-objective human being as part of this Nature." Marx borrowed from Hegel the dialectical schema of self-realization on the path of self-alienation. But for Marx, the subject of this process was not the Absolute, but instead the "real, physical human being, standing on the solid, well-founded earth, exhaling and inhaling all the force of Nature." Marxist materialism is concerned not with matter in the physical and chemical sense, but with man who influences nature through the work process and produces himself out of nature.[153]

It has been proved that Marx not only knew Hegel's *Philosophy of Law,* but even studied it intensively, although strangely enough, Marx never goes into Hegel's criticism of bourgeois society. Hegel's ruthless criticism, whose acerbity was topped only by Marx's, has never been given its due by either historians of philosophy or Marxists. The reason for this, according to Robert Heiss, remains an inexplicable enigma. "Anyone reading Hegel's description of bourgeois society and having even limited knowledge of the basic theses of the late Marx is forced to admit that all the fundamental elements of Marx's thinking are contained in this section of [Hegel's] *Philosophy of Law.*"[154]

Naturally, we ought to remember that Marx borrowed his key

concept of the "dialectical work process" not from Hegel's legal philosophy but from *The Phenomenology of Mind,* specifically the chapter on *Lordship and Bondage,* in which Hegel says that the master possesses actual being-for-itself, whereas the servant, due to his estrangement in work, has merely a being-for-something-else, and is thus the means to an end. As long as Marx dealt with this classical example of Hegelian dialectics, he could not help feeling grateful to and admiring his elder, who (says Marx) advanced to a correct understanding of the essence of work, inasmuch as Hegel viewed it as the dialectical process of "self-production" of man and viewed man as "the product of his own work."[155] Yet a basic error obtains, according to Marx. For Hegel, the subject of the dialectical process is "self-awareness," whereas for Marx, man is its subject. In other words, the Hegelian process of self-awareness is superseded by the relationship between man and nature. The conversion of Hegel's ideas in reference to the dialectics of *Lordship and Bondage* occurs in Marx's equation of work and production: man puts forth something out of himself and lets it become objective reality in nature. "What makes the worst [human] architect superior to the best bee is the fact that he constructs in his head first, while the bee constructs only in wax."[156]

In the work process, the working human being places his essence in the product of his work. The more he alienates his life by putting it into the object, the poorer he becomes; he no longer belongs to himself, but to the thing, the product of his work. The alienation of the worker from the product of his work is for Marx the root of all evil in the life of contemporary society. The alienation of the worker from his work leads to the circumstance that his work appears as something external, which he cannot feel positive about, but negates, and the execution of which does not gladden him, but makes him unhappy. Outside of work, man is himself; at work, man is beside himself. This fact makes obvious the self-alienation of man in paid labor. A further result is the alienation existing between people: as long as the social order remains unchanged, human relations will be perverted and inhuman. Man is not interested in his fellow man as such, but only as an instrument of profit-making for the owners of the means of production, or as an instrument for acquiring income for the worker.[157]

Only the abolition *(Aufhebung)* of private property will enable society to reach that state in which the naturalism of humanity coincides with the humanism of nature. Marx defined communism in the following terms:

". . . as consummate naturalism-humanism, and as consummate humanism-naturalism . . . communism is the true solution to the

Friedrich Engels.

conflict between man and nature as well as between man and man, the true solution to the struggle between existence and essence, between objectivation and self-assertion, between freedom and necessity, between the individual and the species. Communism is the solving of the enigma of history and knows itself as the solution."[158]

Friedrich Engels, too, wanted to employ dialectics to overcome mechanical materialism; he, too, formed his use of the concept by dealing with Hegel. He agrees with Hegel's description of the world as not a complex of finished things, but a complex of processes. Yet Engels felt that Hegel was wrong in seeing dialectics as the self-process of Notion. "It was necessary to abolish this ideological inversion. We regarded the Notions in our head materialistically again as copies of real things rather than considering real things to be copies of some stage of the absolute Notion. . . . In this way, the dialectics of Notion became merely the conscious reflection of the dialectical process of the real world, and thus Hegelian dialectics was turned upside down, or rather, having stood topsy-turvy, it was turned right side up."[159]

Engels completely failed to understand what Hegel meant by "the absolute Idea." According to Hegel's principle of identity, Nature is not to be regarded as a copy of the absolute Idea, but rather as this Idea itself in a different being. Yet the misconception of "copy" was the basis for the controversial "reversal" of Hegelian dialectics into materialistic dialectics. The preceding quotations from Engels contain another great misconception. Only the viewpoint that thinking is derived from nature and that reality does not issue from the Idea can be called materialism. The statement that "our Notions are copies of real things" is not made by materialism, but by a naive, epistemological realism.

The new materialist dialectics is elucidated by Engels in three laws, in which once again Hegelian ideas are "reversed": (1) the law of the conversion of quantity into quality (all development occurs in two phases, an evolutionary and a revolutionary one, at whose end there is a higher quality); (2) the law of the interpenetration of opposites (of the unity and the antithetical struggle between the proletariat and the propertied classes); and (3) the law of negation (every developmental stage attained is negated in the course of further development and replaced by a different form, which however is in turn replaced, that is, sublated).[160]

As we have seen, the basic philosophical position of Marxism can be explained as a reaction against certain insufficiencies in the Hegelian system. Both Marx and Engels believed they had gotten rid of these defects by "reversal." Yet this correction of Hegel by means of "reversal" is—at least methodologically—a dubious affair, made possible, especially in Engels' case, only by a series of misconceptions of Hegelian philosophy. In point of fact, Hegel was not turned upside down; instead, a non-existent theory was turned into its opposite. Any serious criticism of Hegel would have to begin with his monistic principle, but this very fact was disregarded by Marx and particularly by Engels. Hegel never claimed anywhere that reality is "a copy of the absolute Idea," nor is Marx correct when he says that for Hegel "awareness determines social being." After all, Hegelian philosophy does not require its own epistemology to explain the relationship between thinking and being, reality and logic. In dialectical logic, Hegel takes a single principle and from it he develops in rigorous consequence the construction of reality as a cogitated reality. Thus, logic as the study of thinking coincides with ontology as the study of being.

A further example will show how little Marxist criticism dealt with Hegel's monism. Hegel's doctrine that the origin of the spirit is independent of nature implies, according to Engels, the existence of a Christian Creator-God, which implication in itself refutes the doctrine. Yet this refutation is based on oversimplification. Hegel's Christianity is not denied if we point out that this philosophy of identity does not presuppose a "Biblical God," since Hegel identifies Nature with the Creator-Spirit. Christian dogma, on the other hand, sees Nature as the product of the Creator-Spirit and views the Creator and his Creation as essentially different.

Both Hegel and Marx were to some extent considered prophets in their own time. Hegel believed that his philosophy marked the arrival of a sort of historical finality. "When philosophy paints its gray on gray, the form of life has grown old and cannot be rejuvenated with gray on gray but only cognized; it is only when twilight sets in that the owl of Minerva begins to fly." But in the contemporary Prussian State, the goal of world history had not been reached. History proceeded beyond Hegel and his period, taking an unforeseen course. The "cunning of reason" proved itself exactly as Hegel had defined it—against him. Marx was of the opinion that revolution and the socializing of the means of production would suffice to overcome human selfishness and would bring about a classless society and an ideal finality. But we who live today can bear witness that the development of both the western and the eastern worlds has been quite different from what Marx thought it would be. Yet disillusion cannot prevent us from acknowledging the historical power of both Hegel's and Marx's ideas.

Hegel (bas-relief by Drake, 1850).

Chronology

1770 On August 27, Georg Wilhelm Friedrich Hegel is born in Stuttgart, South
Germany. He is the son of Georg Ludwig Hegel (a secretary in the revenue
office and subsequently an expeditionary councilor) and his wife Maria Magdalena, née Fromm.

1773 From his third year until 1775 he attends the German, and then the Latin,
School in his home town.

1780 He transfers to the *Gymnasium Illustre* (subsequently the *Eberhard-Ludwigs-
Gymnasium*) in Stuttgart.

1784 Death of his mother.

1785 He begins keeping a journal in German and Latin.

1788 Graduation from the *Gymnasium*. In the winter semester of 1788–1789, he
begins studying on a scholarship in the Tübingen Seminary. His university
subjects are philosophy and theology.

1790 As of the winter term of 1790–1791, Hegel, Hölderlin, and Schelling share
a room at the *Tübinger Stift*, forming a friendship that crumbled only because of Hölderlin's serious illness and the gradual estrangement of Hegel
and Schelling as of 1807. Hegel is an enthusiastic fan of Rousseau. On September 27, he becomes a Master of Philosophy.

1793 Having passed the Consistorial Examination in theology on September 20, Hegel concludes his studies and goes to Stuttgart for a rest. There he meets G. F. Stäudlein. In October, Hegel accepts a position as tutor in the home of C. F. Steiger von Tschugg in Berne.

1797 Hegel becomes a tutor in Frankfurt am Main. In his *System Fragment,* Hegel drafts his dialectical method. He switches over from theological to political themes.

1799 Death of Hegel's father. Hegel inherits a minor fortune that enables him to prepare for an academic career.

1801 Through the intercession of Schelling, who has been a Professor at Jena since his twenty-third birthday, Hegel receives his post-doctoral *habilitation* at Jena on August 27. His first philosophical work has already appeared: *Difference Between Fichte's and Schelling's Systems of Philosophy.*

1802 Hegel and Schelling found the *Critical Journal of Philosophy.*

1805 Hegel becomes an associate professor of philosophy at Jena, with an annual salary of 100 thalers.

1806 The Battle of Jena. With the final manuscript pages of his fundamental work, *The Phenomenology of Mind,* in his pocket, Hegel flees the city.

1807 Hegel becomes editor of the *Bamberger Zeitung* (Bamberg News).

1808 Hegel becomes Professor of Propaedeutics and Head Master of the *Ägidien Gymnasium* in Nuremberg.

1811 At the age of forty-one, the philosopher marries Marie von Tucher (twenty years old) in Nuremberg.

1812 *The Science of Logic* is published in three volumes.

1816 Hegel becomes a full professor of philosophy at the University of Heidelberg. Besides his usual courses (logic, metaphysics, and natural law), Hegel lectures on aesthetics and history of philosophy.

1817 *The Encyclopedia of the Philosophical Sciences in Outline* is published. In the *Heidelberg Yearbooks for Literature,* Hegel publishes various philosophical and political articles. At the end of the year, *Kultusminister* von Altenstein of Prussia respectfully offers him a professorship at the University of Berlin.

1818 Hegel becomes Fichte's successor in Berlin. He gives his inaugural speech on October 22. He moves into the house at No. 4 *Kupfergraben.*

1820 Hegel becomes a member of the Examining Committee of the Province of Brandenburg. Friction with Schleiermacher.

1821 Hegel's *Philosophy of Law* appears under a double title: *An Outline of Natural Law and Political Science* and *Basic Outline of the Philosophy of Law.* In his courses, he lectures on the philosophy of religion and the philosophy of world history.

1822 A journey to Brussels and the Netherlands.

1824 A journey to Vienna via Prague.

1827 A journey to Paris. On the way back, Hegel visits Goethe in Weimar.

1829 Hegel is at the height of his fame. The influence of the "professor of professors" reaches beyond the borders of Prussia to nearly all German universities. In Berlin, he is elected to the office of University President. That autumn he accidentally meets Schelling in Karlsbad—for the last time.

1831 On November 14, Hegel dies unexpectedly after a brief illness. Two days later, the new University President, Marheineke, delivers the funeral oration in the main hall of the university. Hegel is buried next to Fichte in the Dorotheenstadt Cemetery in Berlin.

Notes

(*Note:* All quotations throughout this volume have been newly translated. Thus no page references can be given for any English edition of the works quoted here, and the following therefore refer to German editions.)

1 *Briefe von und an Hegel* ("Letters from and to Hegel"), Johannes Hoffmeister, Hamburg, 1952–1960, Vol. IV, p. 153.

2 *Documente zu Hegels Entwicklung* ("Documents on Hegel's development"), ed. Johannes Hoffmeister, Stuttgart, 1936, pp. 392 f.

3 J. Klaiber, *Hölderlin, Hegel und Schelling in ihren schwäbischen Jugendjahren* ("Hölderlin, Hegel and Schelling During Their Youth in Swabia"), Stuttgart, 1877, pp. 71 ff; *cf. Briefe,* Vol. IV. p. 157.

4 *Dokumente,* p. 39.

5 K. Fischer, *Hegel's Leben, Werke und Lehre* ("Hegel's Life, Works, and Teachings"), Part I, Heidelberg, 1911, p. 9.

6 *Documente,* p. 8.

7 *Ibid.,* p. 12 f.

8 *Cf.* R. Haym, *Hegel und seine Zeit* ("Hegel and His Time"), Berlin, 1857; reprinted at Hildesheim, 1962, pp. 16 ff.

9 *Documente,* p. 52.

10 *Briefe,* Vol. IV, p. 74.

11 *Cf.* H. Fuhrmans, *F. W. J. Schelling, Briefe und Dokumente* ("Schelling, Letters and Documents"), Vol. I (1775–1809), Bonn, 1962, pp. 9 ff.

12 *Briefe,* Vol. IV, p. 160.

13 *Ibid.,* pp. 162–165.

14 Karl Rosenkranz, *G. W. F. Hegel's Leben* ("Hegel's Life"), Berlin, 1944, p. 30.

15 *Documente,* pp. 433 and 438.

16 *Ibid.,* p. 430.

17 Rosenkranz, pp. 32 ff.

18 *Cf.* Fuhrmans, pp. 34 ff.

19 *Documente,* p. 429.

20 *Theologische Jahrbücher* ("Theological Yearbooks"), Vol. IV (1845), pp. 192 ff.

21 Haym, p. 40.

22 *Documente,* p. 434.

23 *Briefe,* Vol. I, p. 11.

24 *Cf.* F. Bülow, *Hegel. Volk, Staat, Geschichte. Eine Auswahl aus seinen Werken* ("Hegel. Nation, State, History. A Selection from His Works"), Stuttgart, 1942 (Kröners Taschenbuch, Vol. 39), p. 15.

25 *Briefe,* Vol. I, p. 12.

26 *Ibid.,* pp. 16 f.

27 *Ibid.,* pp. 40 f.

28 *Ibid.,* pp. 42 f.

29 *Ibid.,* pp. 45 f.

30 *Ibid.,* pp. 52 f.

31 *Cf.* Rosenkranz, p. 140; Bülow, pp. 23 f.

32 Rosenkranz, p. 141.

33 *Ibid.,* p. 85.

34 *Ibid.,* p. 87.

35 *Briefe,* Vol. I, p. 58.

36 *Ibid.,* pp. 58 ff.

37 Rosenkranz, p. 149.

38 *Ibid.,* pp. 160 and 215.

39 *Ibid.,* p. 218.

40 *Briefe,* Vol. I, p. 68.

41 G. W. Hegel, *Sämtliche Werke: Jubiläumsausgabe in 22 Bänden* ("Complete Works: Jubilee Edition in 22 Volumes"), ed. H. Glockner, 3rd ed., Vol. I, pp. 291 f. (abbreviated hereafter as *SW* I, II, etc.).

42 *Ibid.,* pp. 84 f.

43 *Ibid.,* p. 111.

44 *Cf.* Bülow, p. 48.

45 *Briefe,* Vol. I. p. 119.

46 *Ibid.,* p. 120.

47 *Ibid.,* pp. 131 f.

48 *Ibid.,* p. 134.

49 *Ibid.,* p. 146.

50 *Ibid.,* p. 225.

51 *Ibid.,* p. 225.

52 *Ibid.,* p. 261.

53 *Cf.* Rosenkranz, pp. 247 f.

54 *SW* III, p. 208.

55 *Ibid.,* pp. 313 f.

56 *Cf.* Rosenkranz, pp. 250 f.

57 *Briefe,* Vol. I, p. 356.

58 *Ibid.,* pp. 355 f.

59 *Ibid.,* pp. 367 f.

60 *Ibid.,* p. 359 f.

61 *Briefe,* Vol. III, pp. 434 f.

62 *Briefe,* Vol. IV, pp. 128 f.

63 *Briefe,* Vol. I, pp. 389 f.

64 *Ibid.,* p. 393.

65 *Cf.* H. J. Störig, *Kleine Weltgeschichte der Philosophie* ("Short History of Philosophy"), Stuttgart, 1950, p. 523.

66 *Briefe,* Vol. I, p. 338.

67 *Briefe*, Vol. II, pp. 94 ff.
68 *Ibid.*, pp. 111 f.
69 Quoted by Bülow, p. 53.
70 *Briefe*, Vol. II, pp. 147 f.
71 Fischer, p. 123.
72 Rosenkranz, pp. 302 f.
73 *Briefe*, Vol. II, p. 153.
74 *SW* VI; S. viii.
75 *Cf.* Bülow, pp. 62 f.
76 *Briefe*, Vol. II, p. 197.
77 *Ibid.*, p. 182.
78 *Ibid.*, p. 422.
79 *Ibid.*, p. 170.
80 *Ibid.*, p. 173.
81 *Ibid.*, p. 178.
82 Rosenkranz, p. 319; *cf.* Fischer, p. 140.
83 *Briefe*, Vol. II, p. 189.
84 *Gedenkschrift der Freien Universität Berlin zur 150. Wiederkehr des Gründungsjahres. Idee und Wirklichkeit einer Universität. Dokumente zur Geschichte der Friedrich Wilhelms-Universität zu Berlin* ("Memorial by the Free University of Berlin on the 150th Anniversary of the Founding Year. Idea and Reality of a University. Documents on the History of the Friedrich Wilhelms University of Berlin"), ed. W. Weischedel, Berlin, 1960, p. 309.
85 Bülow, p. 63.
86 *Gedenkschrift*, pp. 310 ff.
87 Quoted by Bülow, p. 65.
88 *Briefe*, Vol. II, p. 218.
89 *Gedenkschrift*, p. 319.
90 *Ibid.*, p. 315.
91 *Ibid.*, p. 325.
92 *Briefe*, Vol. II, p. 221.
93 Quoted by Rosenkranz, pp. 346 f.
94 *Gedenkschrift*, p. 322.
95 *Ibid.*, pp. 319 ff.
96 *SW* XXII, p. 556.
97 Haym, p. 364.
98 *Cf.* Rosenkranz, pp. 336 f.
99 *Ibid.*, p. 335.
100 *SW* XXII, p. 559.
101 Haym, p. 366.
102 *Briefe*, Vol. III, p. 72.
103 R. Heiss, *Die grossen dialektiker des 19. Jahrhunderts. Hegel, Kierkegaard, Marx* ("The Great Dialecticians of the Nineteenth Century. Hegel, Kierkegaard, Marx"), Cologne-Berlin, 1963, pp. 163 and 166 f.
104 *Cf. SW* XXII, p. 561.
105 *Cf.* Haym, pp. 434 f.
106 *SW* XXII, p. 560.
107 Haym, pp. 413 f.
108 *Briefe*, Vol. II, p. 160.
109 *Ibid.*, p. 475.
110 *Briefe*, Vol. II, pp. 204 ff.
111 Quoted by Bülow, pp. 87 f.
112 *Briefe*, Vol. III, p. 278.
113 *Briefe*, Vol. II, p. 316.
114 Fischer, p. 166; *cf. Briefe*, Vol. II, p. 340.
115 *Briefe*, Vol. II, p. 353.
116 *Ibid.*, p. 355.
117 *Ibid.*, pp. 359 f.
118 *Ibid.*, p. 362.
119 - *Ibid.*, pp. 183 ff., 186 ff., 188, 197 f.
120 *Ibid.*, p. 422; Fischer, p. 176.
121 *Briefe*, Vol. II, p. 202.

122 Quoted by Haym, pp. 510 ff.
123 Heinrich von Treitschke, *Deutsche Geschichte des 19. Jahrhunderts* ("German History of the Nineteenth Century"), Leipzig, 1896, Vol. III, p. 721.
124 *Cf.* Fischer, pp. 156–160.
125 *Briefe*, Vol. IV, pp. 117–120.
126 *Briefe* IV, p. 120.
127 Rosenkranz, pp. 355 f. and 360 ff.
128 H. G. Hotho, *Vorstudien für Leben und Kunst* ("Preliminary Study for Life and Art"), Stuttgart and Tübingen, 1835, pp. 388 ff.
129 *Briefe*, Vol. I, p. 194.
130 *Cf.* Fuhrmans, p. 529 ff.
131 *Briefe*, Vol. II, p. 72.
132 Fuhrmans, p. 551.
133 *Briefe*, Vol. III, p. 270.
134 *Ibid.*, pp. 275–280.
135 *Ibid.*, pp. 135 ff.
136 *Ibid.*, p. 402.
137 *SW* XX, pp. 521–544; Rosenkranz, pp. 410 f.
138 Rosenkranz, p. 419· f.
139 *Ibid.*,; pp. 422 ff.
140 *Gedenkschrift*, pp. 419–422.
141 *Cf.* Störig, p. 557.
142 *Die Hegelsche Rechte. Texte aus den Werken* ("The Hegelian Right Wing. Texts from Their Works"), selection and introduction by Lübbe, Stuttgart-Bad Cannstatt, 1962, pp. 9 f.
143 W. Moog, *Hegel und die Hegelsche Schule* ("Hegel and the Hegelian School"), Munich, 1930, pp. 432 f.
144 *Cf.* Moog, pp. 438 ff.
145 Ludwig Feuerbach, *Sämtliche Werke* ("Complete Works"), Stuttgart, 1908, Vol. VIII, p. 28 f.
146 *Cf.* Moog, p. 465.
147 Quoted by Moog, p. 467.
148 *Cf.* Moog, pp. 482–487.
149 V. I. Lenin, *Ausgewählte Werke* ("Selected Works"), Berlin, 1959. Vol. I, pp. 7 f.
150 *Cf.* G. Wetter, *Die Umkehrung Hegel. Grundzuge und Ursprünge der Sowjetphilosophie* ("The Reversal of Hegel. Basic Features and Origins of Soviet Philosophy"), Cologne, 1963, pp. 9 f.
151 *Cf.* J. Y. Calvez, *Karl Marx. Darstellung und Kritik seines Denkens* ("Karl Marx. Presentation and Critique of his Ideas"), Olten and Freiburg im Breisgau, 1964, pp. 15 f.
152 *Marx-Engels-Gesamt-Ausgabe* ("The Complete Works of Marx and Engels") I, p. 234, Frankfurt (and later Berlin), 1927 ff.
153 Karl Marx, *Die Frühschriften* ("Early Writings"), Stuttgart, 1953, p. 273; *cf.* Wetter, p. 14.
154 Heiss, p. 162.
155 Marx, p. 269.
156 Karl Marx, *Das Kapital* ("Capital"), Hamburg, 1922, Vol. I, p. 140; *cf.* Wetter, pp. 17 f.
157 *Cf.* Wetter, p. 21.
158 Marx, *Die Frühschriften*, p. 235.
159 Marx-Engels, *Ausgewählte Schriften* ("Selected Writings"), Berlin, 1961, Vol. II, pp. 360 f.
160 Friedrich Engels, *Anti-Dühring*, Moscow, 1946, pp. 146 f.; English-language edition published by the same publishing house (Foreign Languages Publishing House, Moscow), 1959.

Bibliography

I. Hegel's Works in English translation.

1. *Early Theological Writings,* tr. T. M. Knox (University of Chicago Press, Chicago, 1948).
2. *The Phenomenology of Mind,* tr., with an Introduction and notes, J. B. Baillie (2nd rev. ed., George Allen & Unwin, London; The Macmillan Co., New York, 1931).
3. *Science of Logic,* tr. W. H. Johnstone and L. G. Struthers (2 vols., George Allen & Unwin, London, 1929).
4. *The Logic of Hegel,* tr. William Wallace, (2nd rev. ed., Clarendon Press, Oxford, 1892).
5. *Philosophy of Right,* tr., with notes, T. M. Knox (Clarendon Press, Oxford, 1942).
6. *Hegel's Political Writings,* tr. T. M. Knox, with an introductory essay by Z. A. Pelcynski (Clarendon Press, Oxford, 1964).
7. *Lectures on the Philosophy of History,* tr., 1858, from the 3rd German ed., J. Sibree (Dover).
8. *Lectures on the Philosophy of Religion,* Together With a Work on the Proofs of the Existence of God, tr., from the 2nd German ed., the Rev. E. B. Speirs, B. D., & J. Burdon Sanderson (3 vols., Kegan Paul, Trench, Trübner, & Co., London, 1895).
9. *Lectures on the History of Philosophy,* tr. Elizabeth S. Haldane and Frances Simson (Kegan Paul, Trench, Trübner, & Co., London, 1892-96).
10. *The Philosophy of Fine Art,* tr. F. P. B. Osmaston (4 vols., G. Bell & Sons, London, 1920).

II. Standard German Editions of Hegel's Works.

1. *Sämtliche Werke: Jubiläumsausgabe in 22 Bänden,* ed. Hermann Glockner (Frommann, Stuttgart, 1927-30).
2. *Sämtliche Werke:* Kritische Ausgabe, ed. Georg Lasson (Felix Meiner, Hamburg, 1955).

III. Selected Critical Works in English.

1. *What is Living and What is Dead of the Philosophy of Hegel?* Benedetto Croce, tr. Douglas Ainslie (3rd Italian ed., Macmillan & Co., Ltd., London, 1915).
2. *Hegel: A Reexamination,* J. N. Findlay (The Macmillan Co., London and New York, 1958).
3. *Hegel,* Reinterpretation, Texts and Commentary. Walter Kaufman (Doubleday & Co., Inc., Garden City, N.Y., 1965). Includes previously untranslated correspondence and other new and interesting material on Hegel's life and early influences.
4. *Reason and Revolution:* Hegel and the Rise of Social Theory, Herbert Marcuse (2nd ed., Oxford University Press, 1941).
5. *An Introduction to Hegel,* G. R. G. Mure (Clarendon Press, Oxford, 1940).
6. *The Philosophy of Hegel,* A Systematic Exposition, W. T. Stace (Macmillan & Co., Ltd., London, 1924).

Index

Abel, Jakob Friedrich von, 16
Altenstein, Karl Sigmund Franz vom Stein zum, 62 f, 77, 79, 93, 113
Altenstein, Fräulein vom Stein zum, 65
Aristotele, 50
Augusti, Johann Christian Wilhelm, 34
Autenrieth, Johann Christoph Friedrich, 23

Bacon, Francis, 78
Bähr, Karl Wilhelm Christian, 13
Baillie, Sir James Black, 121
Barez, 109
Bauer, Bruno, 115, 117, 124
Bauer, Edgar, 119
Baur, Ferdinand Christian, 117
Bekker, August Immanuel, 93
Beneke, Friedrich Eduard, 93 f
Billing, André, 20
Bloch, August Friedrich, 104
Böckh, August, 93
Boisserée, Sulpiz, 62, 83
Bök, August Friedrich, 16, 23
Bolland, Gerardus J. P. J., 121
Borelius, 121
Bosanquet, Bernard, 121
Breyer, Karl Wilhelm Friedrich, 18, 20
Bülow, Friedrich, 60
Burke, Edmund, 12
Burkhardt, Christiana Charlotte, 40, 48
Burkhardt, Georg Ludwig Friedrich; see Ludwig Fischer

Caird, Edward, 121
Caird, John, 121
Carové, Friedrich Wilhelm, 57, 65, 114

Christoph, Herzog von Württemberg, 12
Correggio, Antonio Allegri, 90
Cousin, Victor, 57, 89–90 f, 121
Creuzer, Georg Friedrich, 55, 60, 63, 71, 75
Croce, Benedetto, 121

Daub, Karl, 52, 55, 60, 103
Descartes, René, 45, 81
Diez, 20
Donhoff, K., 9
Donzelli, Domenico, 89
Duttenhofer, Christian Friedrich, 11, 20

Ebbinghaus, Julius, 121
Echtermeyer, Theodor, 118
Eckerlin, 89
Eckermann, Johann Peter, 85
Endel, Nanette, 28
Engels, Friedrich, 115, 122, 127 f
d'Ercole, 121
Erdmann, Johann Eduard, 93, 114
Eschenburg, Johann Joachim, 11
Eschenmayer, Philipp Kaspar Heinrich, 55
Eyck, Jan van, 88

Faber, Jonathan Heinrich, 19
Fallot, 17, 20
Feder, 13
Ferguson, Adam, 13
Feuerbach, Ludwig, 115, 118–120 f, 125
Fichte, Johann Gottlieb, 20, 24, 25, 26, 31, 32, 35 f, 45, 53, 63, 66, 72, 75 f, 81, 101, 110, 113, 115, 118, 120
Filmer, 79

Finck, 17, 23
Fischer, Kuno, 13, 66, 114
Fischer, Ludwig, 40, 48–49 f
Flatt, Johann Friedrich, 16, 20
Fodor, Joséphine, 89 f
Förster, Friedrich Christoph, 103, 104, 111
Frederick II, the Great, 95
Friedrich Wilhelm III, 62, 113 f, 114
Friederich Wilhelm IV, 102, 113
Fries, Jakob Friedrich, 31, 53, 76–77 f
Fromm, Maria Magdalena; *see* Maria Magdalena Hegel
Frommann, Karl Friedrich Ernst, 42, 48, 102

Gabler, Georg Andreas, 117
Gabler, *Prorektor,* 39
Gans, Eduard, 79, 96, 103, 104, 107 f, 114, 124
Garve, Christian, 13
Gentile, Giovanni, 121
Ghert, Peter Gabriel van, 87, 88, 91, 121
Glockner, Hermann, 60, 78, 83, 108, 121
Goebhardt, Joseph Anton, 37
Goethe, August von, 84–86 f
Goethe, Johann Wolfgang von, 31, 35, 36 f, 37, 49, 83–84 f, 104, 105, 107
Goethe, Ottilie von, 85
Gogel, Johann Noë, 27
Gontard, Jakob Friedrich, 27
Gontard, Susanna, 27
Göschel, Karl Friedrich, 116, 117
Green, Thomas Hill, 121
Griesinger, Georg Friedrich, 12
Grotius, Hugo (Huig de Groot), 25

Haller, Karl Ludwig von, 79
Hammacher, Emil, 121
Hartwig, Aimée von, 103
Hauber, Karl Friedrich, 20
Hauff, Wilhelm, 14
Haym, Rudolf, 23, 76, 77, 78, 79 f, 82, 92
Hegel, Christiane Luise, 10, 11, 28, 30, 46, 61, 108
Hegel, Georg Ludwig (father), 10, 11, 15 f, 22, 24, 30
Hegel, Georg Ludwig (son), 10, 48, 49
Hegel, Immanuel, 48, 49, 107, 111
Hegel, Johannes, 9
Hegel, Johannes (pastor), 9
Hegel, Karl, 48, 107, 111

Hegel, Maria Magdalena Louisa, 9, 11, 12, 30
Hegel, Marie, 45, 46–49 f, 55, 56, 64, 79, 84, 87, 89, 94 f, 95, 102, 103, 108 f
Heiberg, Johan Ludvig, 121
Heiss, Robert, 79, 125
Hemsterhuis, Franz, 19
Henning, Leopold Dorotheus von, 65, 71, 75
Herbart, Johann Friedrich, 24, 120
Herder, Johann Gottfried von, 19
Hermes, Johann Thimotheus, 13
Hinrichs, Hermann Friedrich Wilhelm, 57, 74, 75, 114
Hobbes, Thomas, 25, 79
Hoffmeister, Johannes, 121
Höijer, 121
Hölderlin, Friedrich, 17, 18, 23, 24, 26, 27 f, 28 f
Homer, 13
Horn, Dr., 109
Hotho, Heinrich Gustav, 81, 97, 103, 104
Hufeland, Christoph Wilhelm, 35
von Hülsen, 104
Hume, David, 25, 45

Jacobi, Friedrich Heinrich, 19, 35, 57, 60, 76, 77, 102
Jean Paul (Jean Paul Friedrich Richter), 12
Jesus Christ, 74, 117 f

Kalb, Charlotte von, 27
Kamptz, Karl Christoph Albert Heinrich von, 104
Kant, Immanuel, 19, 20 f, 21, 24, 29, 35, 37, 45 f, 53, 76, 77, 115, 120
Karl August, Grand Duke of Saxe-Weimar, 84
Karl Eugen, Duke of Württemberg, 21
Kästner, Abraham Gotthelf, 13
Kierkegaard, Sören, 81
Klaiber, Julius, 16
Knebel, Karl Ludwig von, 39, 86
Köppen, Karl Friedrich, 124
Köstlin, Karl Reinhold, 121
Kotzebue, August Friedrich Ferdinand von, 73
Krause, Karl Christian Friedrich, 31, 94

Lablache, Luigi, 89
Lasson, Adolf, 121

Lasson, Georg, 48, 121
Lebret, Johann Friedrich, 23
Leibniz, Gottfried Wilhelm, 25, 45
Lenin, Vladimir I., 122
Leo, Heinrich, 118 f
Leonardo da Vinci, 90
Leutwein, Christian Philipp, 20, 22
Link, Herbert, 53
Litt, Theodor, 121
Locke, John, 25, 45
Löffler, 11, 13
Lübbe, Hermann, 115
Luther, Martin, 93, 95, 106

Machiavelli, Niccolò, 25
Malebranche, Nicolas de, 45
Marcus, Adalbert Friedrich, 101
Marheineke, Philipp Konrad, 75, 107, 111, 117
Marino, 121
Märklin, Jakob Jeremias Friedrich, 18, 20, 22 f
Marx, Karl, 115, 116 f, 119, 122–129 f
McTaggart, John McTaggart Ellis, 121
Mehmel, Gottlob Ernst August, 52
Mercadante, Giuseppe Saverio Raffaele, 89
Michelet, Karl Ludwig, 114, 117, 118, 121
Milder-Hauptmann, Pauline Anna, 89 f
Monrad, 121
Montesquieu, Charles de Secondat, Baron de, 19, 25
Montgelas, Maximilian Count von, 39
Moses, 45

Napoleon I, 37, 38, 55, 90
Neuffer, Christian Ludwig, 20, 28
Newton, Sir Isaac, 83
Nicolai, Christoph Friedrich, 13
Niebuhr, Barthold Georg, 53
Niethammer Friedrich Immanuel, 35, 37 f, 40 f, 45, 48, 49, 50, 52, 60, 102
Nohl, Herman, 28
Novalis (Baron Friedrich von Hardenberg), 35

Oppenheim, 114
Ott, 121

Paulus, Elisabeth Friederike Caroline, 55
Paulus, Heinrich Eberhard Gottlob, 35, 52, 55, 56, 60, 101

Pelargus, Wilhelm, 10
Pfaff, Johann Friedrich, 52 f
Plato, 19, 45
Pogwisch, Ulrike von, 85
Prevost, 121

Raphael (Raffaello Santi), 90
Ranke, Leopold von, 114
Rauch, Christian Daniel, 104
Raumer, Friedrich Ludwig Georg von, 53
Rebstock, 73
Reinhard, Karl Friedrich von, 84
Reinhold, Karl Leonhard, 20, 26, 32
Riemer, Friedrich Wilhelm, 84
Röschlaub, Andreas, 101
Rösel, Johann Gottlob Samuel, 104
Rosenkranz, Karl, 13, 20, 29, 42, 44, 45, 60, 65, 74, 76, 77, 95, 106, 114, 116, 117, 121
Rössler, 114
Roth, Karl Johann Friedrich, 102
Rousseau, Jean-Jacques, 16, 19 f, 20, 21
Rubens, Peter Paul, 88
Rubini, Giovanni Battista, 89
Ruge, Arnold, 118, 119
von Rütte, 24 f

Sand, Karl Ludwig, 73
Savigny, Friedrich Carl von, 75, 114, 124
Schad, Johann Baptist, 31
Schaller, Julius, 118
Schelling, Caroline von, 45, 102
Schelling, Friedrich Wilhelm Joseph von, 14, 18, 20, 21, 25 f, 31 f, 35 f, 39 f, 45, 53, 57, 60, 79, 86, 100, 101–102 f, 112, 113 f, 115, 117, 118, 120, 125
Schelling, Karl Eberhard, 45
Schiller, Friedrich, 9 f, 15, 16, 19, 27, 31, 35
Schlegel, August Wilhelm von, 31, 35
Schlegel, Caroline; *see* Caroline von Schelling
Schlegel, Friedrich von, 31
Schleiermacher, Friedrich Ernst Daniel, 62, 72 f, 76, 116
Schnurrer, Christian Friedrich von, 16, 24
Schoeps, Hans Joachim, 52
Scholl, Johann Eberhard Heinrich, 24
Schopenhauer, Arthur, 13, 72

Schröckh, Johann Matthias, 13
Schuckmann, Caspar Friedrich Freiherr von, 53, 77, 89
Schultz, Christoph Friedrich Ludwig, 84
Schulze, Johannes, 71, 92, 93, 110, 111
Schwegler, 20
Schwendler, Friedrich Christian August von, 85
Schwendler, Frau von, 85
Seth, 121
Shaftesbury, Anthony Ashley-Cooper, Earl of, 25
Shakespeare, William, 11
Smith, Adam, 13
Solger, Karl Wilhelm Ferdinand, 53, 66, 72, 95, 110
Sophocles, 66
Spaventa, Bertrando, 121
Spinoza, Benedictus de, 25, 45, 53
Stahl, Friedrich Julius (Friedrich Julius Jolson), 79
Stäudlin, Gotthold Friedrich, 23
Steiger von Tschugg, Carl Friedrich, 24, 25
Steiger von Tschugg, Friedrich, 25
Stein, Karl Reichsfreiherr vom und zum, 62, 76
Stieglitz, Heinrich Wilhelm August, 104
Stirling, James Hutchison, 121
Stirner, Karl, 120
Storr, Gottlob Christian, 16
Strauss, David Friedrich, 114, 117–118 f
Sulzer, Johann Georg, 13

Tieck, Ludwig, 35, 66, 72
Titian (Tiziano Vecelli), 90
Treitschke, Heinrich von, 93

Tucher von Simmelsdorf, Jobst Wilhelm Karl Baron von, 45
Tucher von Simmelsdorf, Marie von; *see* Marie Hegel
Tucher von Simmelsdorf, Susanna Baroness von, 45

Ulrich, Duke of Württemberg, 16
Uxkull, Baron Boris, 57, 59

Varnhagen von Ense, Karl August, 48, 105, 116
Vatke, Johann Karl Wilhelm, 117, 118
Vera, Augusto, 121
Virchow, Rudolf, 112
Vischer, Friedrich Theodor, 118
Vischer, Luise, 9
Vogel, Karl, 85
Voltaire (François-Marie Arouet), 25
Voss, Johann Heinrich, 81

Wahl, Frau von, 103
Wallace, William, 121
Wette, Wilhelm Martin Leberecht de, 53, 73, 75, 76
Wetzel, Friedrich Gottlob, 21
Wichmann, Ludwig Wilhelm, 104
Wilhelm I, King of Württemberg, 60
Winckelmann, Johann Joachim, 71
Windelband, Wilhelm, 121
Wolff, Christian Baron von, 45

Xeller, Christian, 107

Zeller, Eduard, 23
Zelter, Karl Friedrich, 84, 85, 94, 103, 104, 107

Sources of Illustrations

Schiller-Nationalmuseum (National Schiller Museum), Marbach on the Neckar, Germany: Front cover, 11, 38, 51, 123, 131.

Archiv für Kunst und Geschicte (Archive for Art and History), Berlin: 7, 96.

Ullstein Bilderdienst (Ullstein Picture Service), Berlin: 10, 47, 65, 70, 105, 110.

Städtisches Kulturamt (Municipal Cultural Department), Tübingen, Germany: 18.

Historisches Bildarchiv Lolo Handke (Lolo Handke's Historical Picture Archive), Bad Berneck, Germany: 19, 21, 26, 33, 101.

Historia-Photo, Bad Sachsa, Germany: 43, 67, 70, 82, 115.

Hegel Archiv, Bonn, Germany: 58.

Internationaal Instituut voor Sociale Geschiedenis (International Institute of Social History), Amsterdam, Holland: 124, 127.